Combined and Revised

all the GAMES kids like

by Dianne Schoenfeld Barad

100 Reproducible Game Sheets for Speech and Language Therapy

Communication Skill Builders ®

3130 N. Dodge Blvd./P.O. Box 42050
Tucson, Arizona 85733
(602) 323-7500

Duplicating

You may prefer to copy the designated reproducible materials by using stencils or spirit masters. It is not necessary to tear pages out of this book. Make a single photocopy of the desired page. Use this photocopy to make a stencil or spirit master on a thermal copier.

Originally published as *Games Kids Like*, ©1974, *More Games Kids Like*, ©1975, and *Still More Games Kids Like*, ©1981 by Communication Skill Builders, Inc.

©1983 by

**Communication
Skill Builders, Inc.**
3130 N. Dodge Blvd./P.O. Box 42050
Tucson, Arizona 85733
(602) 323-7500

ISBN 0-88450-876-5   Catalog No. 7013

10 9 8 7 6 5 4 3 2
Printed in the United States of America

*To my husband, Phil, for his counsel, patience,
and encouragement in all my endeavors.*

About the Author

Dianne Schoenfeld Barad holds a B.S. from New York University, School of Education. While working as a Speech, Language, and Hearing Specialist in private practice in Los Angeles, she received an M.A. from California State University at Northridge. Ms. Barad also holds the C.C.C. in Speech from the American Speech-Language-Hearing Association.

Ms. Barad's career has extended from New York to California, including positions in Texas and Illinois. Teachers, speech pathologists, and language- and hearing-disabled children and adults have benefited from her programs, demonstrations, and publications.

Currently Ms. Barad is a Speech and Language Specialist at the Bartlett Learning Center in Illinois.

Other products by Dianne Schoenfeld Barad available from Communication Skill Builders:

Un "Familiar" Fables for /s/ Carryover (1979)

Speech News (Revised) (1983)

Words and Sounds Ahoy! (1983)

Talk It Up (1984)

Contents

Introduction

All the Games Kids Like is a compilation of *Games Kids Like, More Games Kids Like,* and *Still More Games Kids Like.* One hundred activities reinforce concepts taught for articulation therapy and language remediation. The activities are suitable for children from kindergarten through eighth grade, for learning-disabled students and for developmentally delayed students. Some of the activities are appropriate for aphasic adults. The game sheets are complete with behavioral objectives and instructions.

These materials were originally designed for the busy speech and language clinician who has a heavy caseload and needs prepared reproducible activities that are also portable and flexible. Over the past ten years the games have demonstrated success not only in the therapy setting but in special-education classes and in regular classrooms. In this revision, some of the original games have been deleted and new games have been added. Behavioral objectives and instructions have been rewritten and extended for greater flexibility.

Typically, the speech and language clinician has a minimal amount of preparation time but a large and varied caseload. *All the Games Kids Like* is a time-saving aid. You select the desired game sheets and duplicate the quantity desired. Some of the games already have stimuli on them. For those that don't, you can quickly jot down the necessary stimuli on each sheet.

Carryover materials are extremely valuable when they can make the transition from therapy to home or school. Game sheets started in a therapy situation may go home with a client for further practice or sent to a teacher for reinforcement in the classroom. Parents and teachers have expressed appreciation for having activities that provide awareness of the content of therapy sessions as well as a structured activity for helping the child.

It is not possible to cover in one volume all the flexible aspects and uses of these game sheets. How to Use These Game Sheets and Game-Sheet Stimuli, on the following pages, will give you some ideas. However, innovation is the key to success. Experiment freely with the materials according to the needs of your clients or students. Use your own ideas and those of your students to adapt these games to individual situations. You'll soon discover that *All the Games Kids Like* is effective and enjoyable for both you and your students.

How to Use These Game Sheets

1. Be sure the players understand what is expected. Before beginning a game, review the material and give clear directions for using the game sheet.

2. When working with a group, the players do not need identical game sheets. The game sheets may be programmed to fit individual objectives. One player may be working with antonyms while another is concentrating on forming questions.

3. If you are working with a group and you want each participant to have identical game sheets, write the stimulus words on a copy of the sheet before duplicating it.

4. Rules given in the instructions are not absolute. They may be changed to suit the situation or individual. Going back a space as a result of an incorrect response might be changed to getting another chance to respond correctly. You may want to eliminate the action of one player "bumping" another player back to *start*.

5. Be flexible. Both the stimuli and the methods of play can be adapted. In some cases, game sheets and instructions may be exchanged, using the instructions from one game with a different game sheet. Spinner boards are often interchangeable. The 1-6 Spinner allows more responses than the 1-4 Spinner. The Plus and Minus Spinner provides more repetition of target-sound stimuli.

6. When sending game sheets home or to the classroom teacher, include a copy of the directions, checking off the objective and the appropriate method of play. Both parents and teachers who work with the student appreciate guidance and clarification.

7. Some students do not fare well under the pressure of competition. For these students, or for a change in routine, the activities may be used as worksheets for written work or for individual oral work with the teacher or an aide.

Game-Sheet Stimuli

Stimulus-response pairs exist in almost unending combinations. A few categories are listed here.

1. **Target Sounds:** When a sound is to be practiced in isolation, you don't have to write the stimuli on the game sheet. The player will produce the same sound for every turn. When the target sound is to be used in words or sentences, the various stimulus words should be written on the game sheet.

2. **Antonyms and Synonyms:** Players provide words that will pair with stimulus words. For antonyms, if the stimulus is *hot*, the player responds *cold*. For synonyms, if the stimulus is *chair*, the response could be *seat*.

3. **Rhyming Words:** A player provides a word that rhymes with the stimulus word. If you have written *fry* as a stimulus, the response might be *cry*.

4. **Question Words:** A player forms a question using the stimulus words *who, what, where, when, why,* and *how*. Forms of *be* and *do* may also be used.

5. **Nouns—Questions:** Players form questions using nouns as stimulus words. If the stimulus is *zoo*, the response could be, "Where is the zoo?" or, "Why did you go to the zoo?"

6. **Nouns—Adjectives:** Players provide adjectives that suitably describe stimulus nouns. If the stimulus is *ice cream*, descriptive words could be *delicious, cold, frozen, flavored.*

7. **Nouns—Plurals:** A player provides the plural form of the stimulus word. If the stimulus is *child*, the response is *children.*

8. **Verb Tenses:** The present form of a verb is the stimulus word. A player responds with the past tense. If the stimulus is *break*, the response is *broke.*

If you prefer stimulus cards to writing stimuli on the game sheets, write stimulus words on 3″ × 5″ cards. Place a stack of the cards in the center of the game activity. For each turn and at the appropriate point in the game, a player turns over a card and responds to the stimulus on that card. Write each stimulus category on different colors. Antonyms might be on pink cards, adjectives on green cards, and classification categories on white cards. For articulation practice, write words containing identical target sounds on cards of the same color. Thus, all words with **R** would be on yellow cards, **S** words could be on pink cards, and **L** words on blue cards.

All the Games Kids Like
K-2

1
Lollipop Climb

Suggested Grade Level: K-2

Materials: Game sheet and crayon or pencil for each player.

Objectives: 1. The student will discriminate a correct versus an incorrect production of a target sound.

2. The student will improve auditory sequential memory, auditory association, and auditory reception.

Method of Play

For Objective 1: Give each player a game sheet and crayon or pencil. Starting at the bottom of the lollipop, players mark a space each time they hear a correct production of the target sound. Target sounds may be given correctly and incorrectly in syllables, words, phrases, or sentences. Play stops when all spaces have been marked.

For Objective 2: Give each player a game sheet and a crayon or pencil. Tell the players that they are going to climb up the lollipop. Stimuli are provided orally:

   a. Numbers, words, lists, or sentences to recall.

   b. Word associations.

      Example: Shoes and _____ .

   c. Questions requiring specific responses.

      Example: Are ice cubes hot?
               What do you wear on your head?

Players take turns responding. If a response is correct, the player, starting at the bottom, marks a space on the game sheet. The object is to mark all spaces on the game sheet.

1 Lollipop Climb

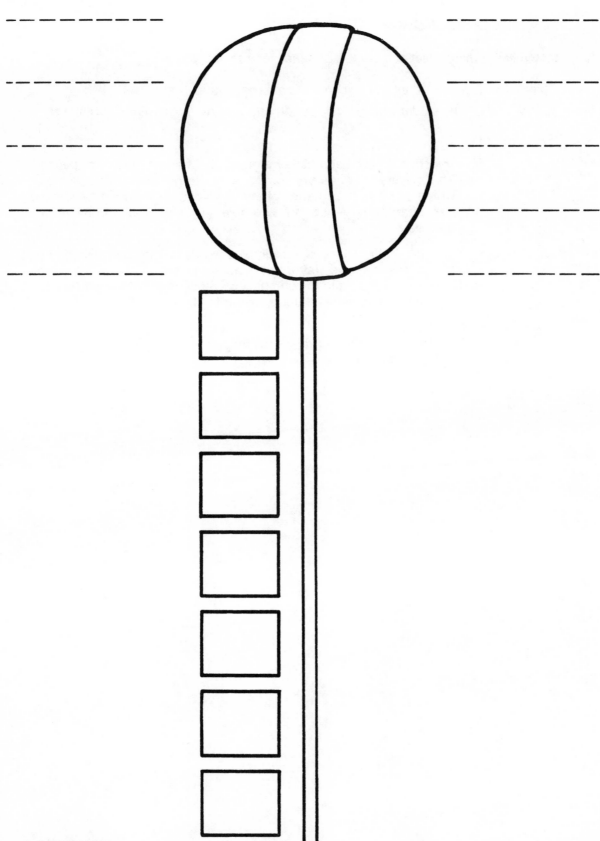

2
The Pear Tree

Suggested Grade Level: K-2

Materials: Game sheet and crayon or pencil for each player.

Objectives: 1. The student will discriminate a target sound.

  2. The student will provide synonyms, antonyms, rhyming words, etc.

Method of Play

For Objective 1: Give each player a game sheet and a crayon or pencil. The players listen as you produce the target sound in syllables, words, phrases, or sentences. Players color or mark a pear each time they hear the target sound. The object is to color all the pears on the tree.

For Objective 2: Write the desired stimulus words on the pears. Distribute the game sheets and crayons or pencils. Players take turns selecting a pear, responding to the stimulus correctly, and coloring the pear. The object is to color all the pears on the tree.

Variation:
Provide a stimuli orally with players coloring a pear when the response is correct.

2 The Pear Tree

All the Games Kids Like
K-3

3
Balloon Game

Suggested Grade Level: K-3

Materials: Game sheet and crayon or pencil for each player.

Objectives: 1. The student will correctly articulate a target sound.

2. The student will provide adjectives, adverbs, rhyming words, items in a category, etc.

Method of Play

For Objective 1: Write a stimulus word containing the target sound on each balloon. Distribute the game sheets and crayons or pencils. Players take turns selecting a balloon, saying the stimulus word correctly, and coloring the balloon or drawing the string on it. If a production is incorrect, the student waits for the next turn and tries again. The object is to color or mark all the balloons.

For Objective 2: Write the desired stimuli on the balloons. Distribute the game sheets and crayons or pencils. Players take turns selecting a balloon and responding to the stimulus word. If correct, the student colors the balloon or draws a string on it. When working with classification or stimuli where more than one response may be provided, use the 1-4 Spinner to determine the number of responses for each turn.

Variation:
A point may be awarded for each correct response. Total the points at the end of the game to determine the winner.

3 **Balloon Game**

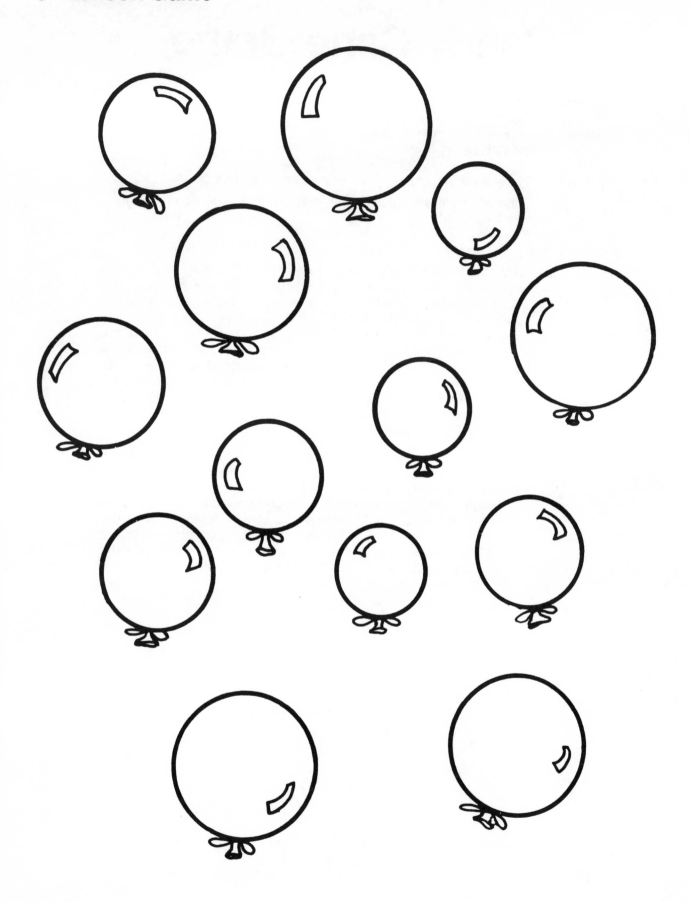

4
Candy Cane Game

Suggested Grade Level: K-3

Materials: Game sheet and marker for each player.
1-4 Spinner.

Objectives: 1. The student will correctly articulate a target sound.

2. The student will use antonyms, synonyms, adjectives, adverbs, plurals, verb tenses, etc.

Method of Play:

For Objective 1: Write stimulus words containing the target sound in the spaces. On the bow, write a more difficult word or words to be used in a sentence. Distribute the game sheets and markers. Each player in turn spins the 1-4 Spinner and moves the indicated number of spaces, saying each stimulus word passed. A correct response allows the player to remain on the space the marker lands on. If a response is incorrect, the player goes back one space. A player landing on the bow receives an extra turn if all the responses are correct. A player reaches the bow either by a direct spin or by landing on a space that says *Go to bow.* The first player to reach the bottom of the cane is the winner.

For Objective 2: Write stimulus words in the spaces with a more difficult stimulus on the bow. Distribute the game sheets and markers. Each player in turn spins the 1-4 Spinner and moves the indicated number of spaces. The player must then respond correctly to the stimulus word on that space. If the response is correct, a point is won. If a player lands on the bow and responds correctly, double points are given. Play continues until all players have reached the bottom of the cane. Total the points. The player with the most points is the winner.

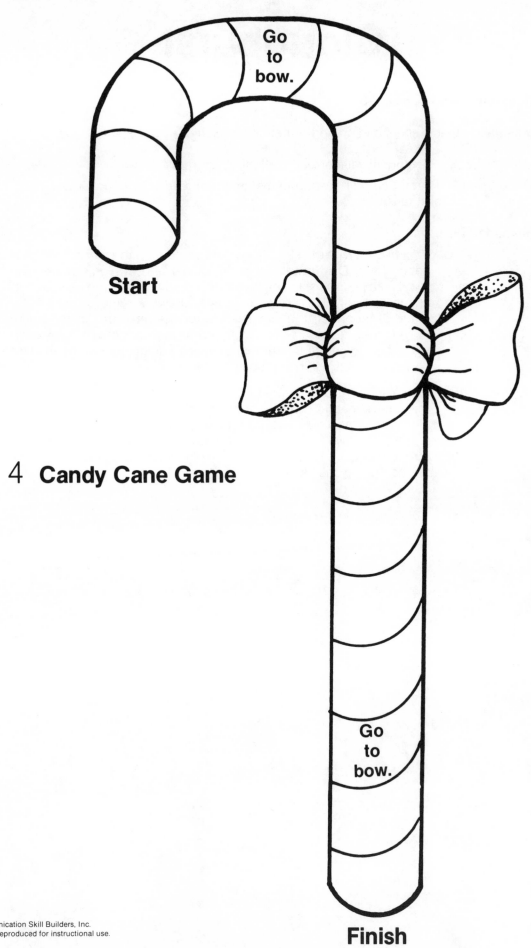

Start

4 Candy Cane Game

Go
to
bow.

Go
to
bow.

Finish

5
Cloudburst

Suggested Grade Level: K-3

Materials: Game sheet and crayon or pencil for each player.

Objectives: 1. The student will correctly articulate a target sound.

2. The student will use antonyms, synonyms, adjectives, adverbs, plurals, past tense, etc.

Method of Play:

For Objective 1: Write the stimulus words containing the target sound on each cloud. Distribute the game sheets and crayons or pencils. Players take turns selecting a cloud and articulating the word in that space correctly. If correct, the player draws a raindrop below the cloud. If incorrect, the player waits for the next turn to try again. Players may be required to use the words in sentences or to say each word a pre-determined number of times. The object is to be the first player to "burst" all the clouds.

For Objective 2: Write the desired stimulus words in the spaces. Distribute the game sheets and crayons or pencils. Each player in turn selects a cloud and responds accordingly. If correct, the player draws a raindrop below the cloud. If incorrect, the player waits for the next turn to try again. Play ends when all players have "burst" the clouds on their game sheets.

5 **Cloudburst**

6
Fishing Game

Suggested Grade Level: K-3

Materials: Game sheet and crayon or pencil for each player.

Objectives: 1. The student will correctly articulate a target sound.
2. The student will use rhyming words, spatial relationships, antonyms, synonyms, definitions, etc.

Method of Play:

For Objective 1: Write stimulus words containing the target sound on the fish. Distribute the game sheets and crayons or pencils. Players take turns selecting a fish and articulating the stimulus word. If correct, they color or mark the fish. If incorrect, they must try again in the next turn. The object of the game is to catch as many fish as possible by saying the stimulus words correctly. Play stops when all fish have been caught.

For Objective 2: Write stimulus words or sentences on the fish. Distribute the game sheets and crayons or pencils. In turn, a player selects a fish and responds to the stimulus. If the response is correct, the player colors the fish while the next player takes a turn. The player catching the most fish wins the game.

Variation:
Stimuli may be provided orally. For example, to practice following instructions, give an instruction. If it is followed accurately, the player catches a fish and colors it.

18

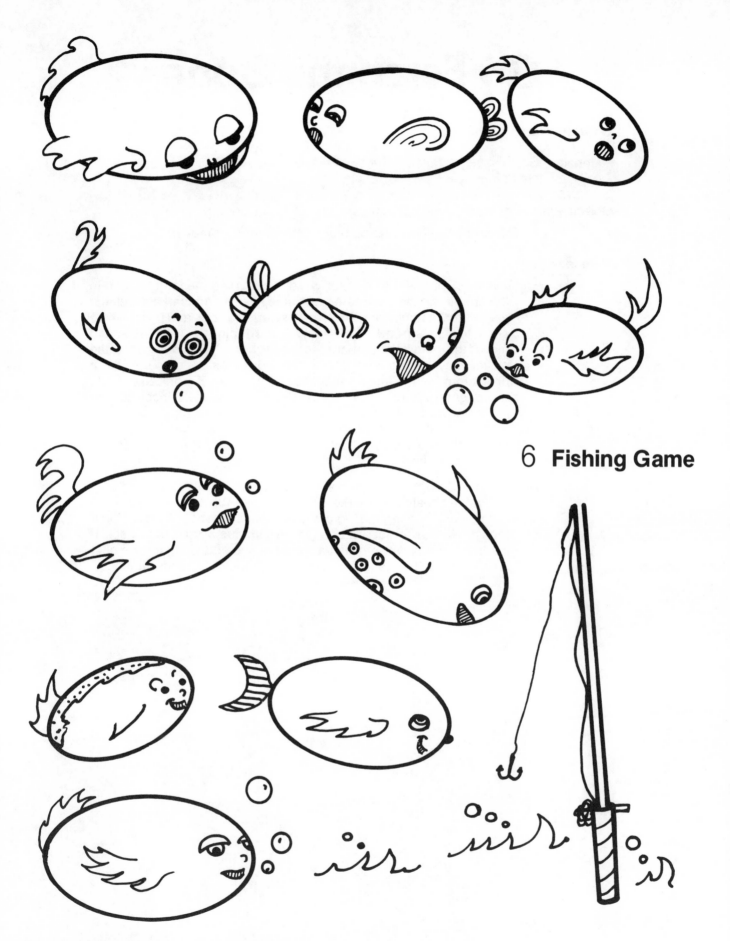

6 **Fishing Game**

7
Go Fetch the Bone

Suggested Grade Level: K-3

Materials: Game sheet and marker for each player.
1-4 Spinner.

Objectives: 1. The student will correctly articulate a target sound.

            2. The student will provide antonyms, synonyms, homonyms, etc.

Method of Play:

For Objective 1: Write the stimulus words containing the target sound in the empty spaces. Distribute the game sheets and markers. Tell the players that a puppy named *Shep* has buried a bone and that they are going to help him find it. Each player in turn spins the 1-4 Spinner and moves the indicated number of spaces. When landing on a space, the player may be required to use the word in a sentence, say it a pre-determined number of times, or just say it correctly. If the response is correct, the player remains on that space. If incorrect, the player moves back one space and responds to that stimulus word. A player landing on a space containing another student's marker *bumps* the other player back to *Start.* The first player to reach the bone is the winner.

For Objective 2: Write the desired stimulus words in the spaces. Distribute the game sheets and markers. Players take turns spinning the 1-4 Spinner and moving the indicated number of spaces. A player must then provide a correct response to the stimulus word in that space. If incorrect, the player moves back one space and waits for the next turn to try again. The first player to reach the bone is the winner.

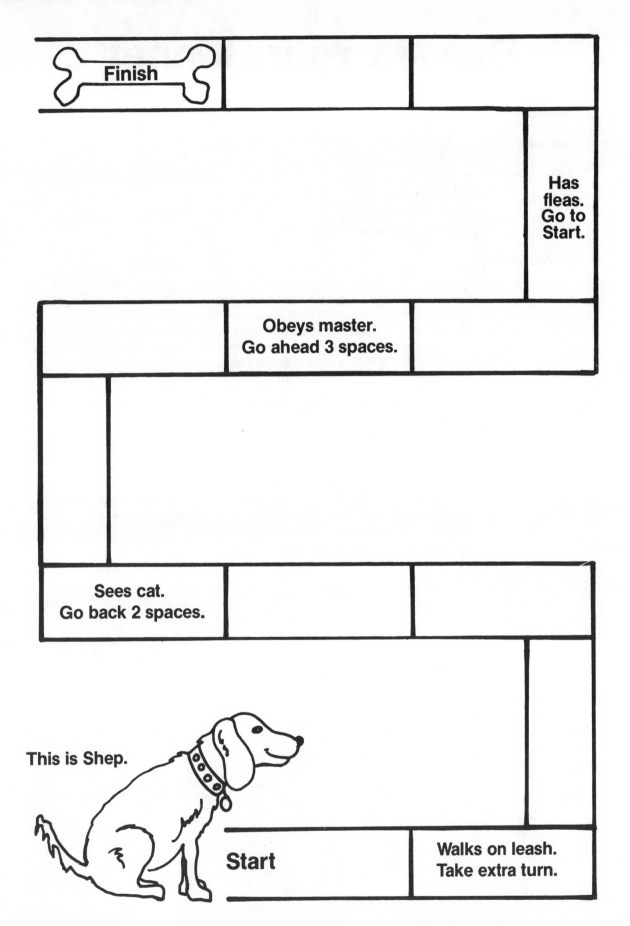

Finish

Has fleas. Go to Start.

Obeys master. Go ahead 3 spaces.

Sees cat. Go back 2 spaces.

This is Shep.

Start

Walks on leash. Take extra turn.

8
Bees in Your Bonnet

Suggested Grade Level: K-3

Materials: Game sheet and crayon or pencil for each player.

Objectives: 1. The student will differentiate between a correct versus an incorrect production of a target sound.

2. The student will differentiate between antonyms, synonyms, rhyming words, or other paired associates.

Method of Play:

For Objective 1: Distribute game sheets and crayons or pencils. Tell players to listen while you make the sound. Whenever the target sound is articulated correctly, players mark a bee on the game sheet. Whenever the sound is misarticulated, players make a mark on the hat. Present the sounds to be discriminated in random order and change them as often as necessary. The game ends when players are able to make the differentiation with consistency.

For Objective 2: Distribute game sheets and crayons or pencils. Ask the stimulus question and be sure the players understand it.

Examples: "Are these words synonyms?"
"Do these words rhyme?"
"Do these words have the same initial consonant?"

Tell players to listen while you say two words. If the words match, players mark a bee. If the words do not match, players make a mark on the hat. The game ends when the players are responding correctly consistently or at your discretion.

8 Bees in Your Bonnet

9
Sounds the Flowers Make

Suggested Grade Level: K-3

Materials: Game sheet and crayon or pencil for each player.

Objectives: 1. The student will differentiate between similar sounds.

2. The student will differentiate between paired associates such as rhyming words, vowels, and consonants in words and sentences with only minor differences.

Method of Play:

For Objective 1: Write a different stimulus sound on each flower pot. Distribute the game sheets and crayons or pencils. Tell players what the sound is on each pot. When you produce one of the sounds, each player locates the correct pot and draws a flower on one of its branches. Play continues until each branch has a flower on it.

For Objective 2: Give each player a game sheet and a crayon or pencil. Say two associated words. If the players hear the association, they draw a flower on a branch in any pot. If the stimuli are not associates, players draw a leaf.

Examples: Cat and *bat* rhyme, so each player draws a flower.
Cat and *tap* do not rhyme, so each player draws a leaf.

This can also be done in sentences.

Examples: Mom wanted to bake a cake.
Mom wanted to take a cake.

This game will work with identical vowel or consonant sounds in a given position.

Examples: bear, boast (initial)
egg, bag (final)
borrow, carry (medial)

The game ends when all branches are filled with flowers and leaves.

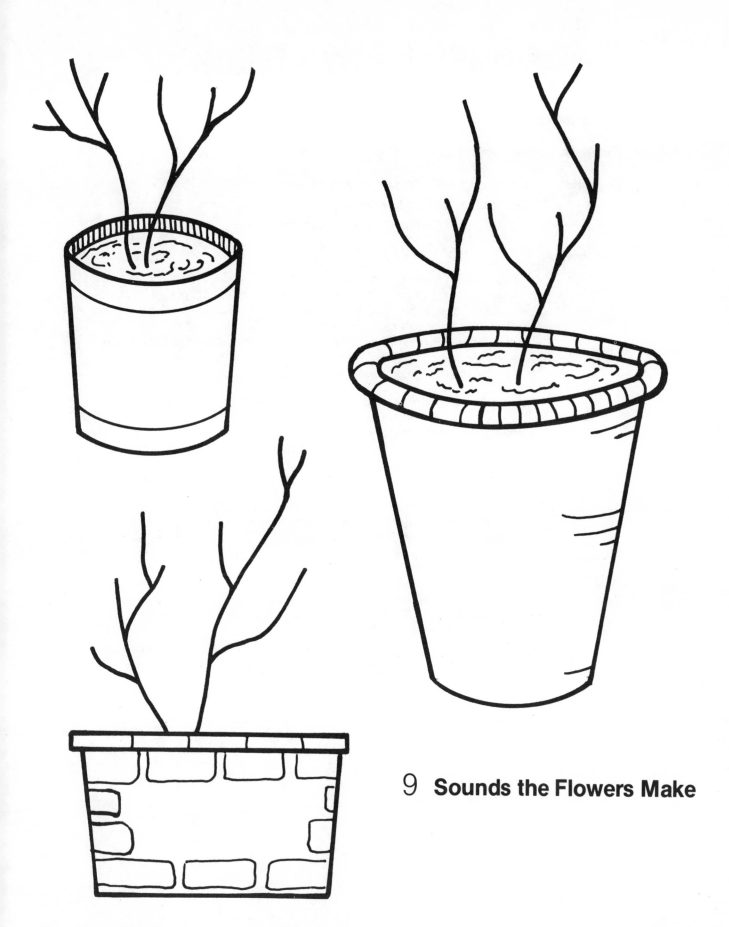

9 **Sounds the Flowers Make**

10
What's in the Sack?

Suggested Grade Level: K-3

Materials: Game sheet and a crayon or pencil for each player.

Objectives: 1. The student will correctly articulate a target sound.

2. The student will classify items.

3. The student will improve auditory association.

Method of Play:

For Objective 1: Tell the players they will be timed while "filling" a sack with objects that contain their target sounds. Give each player a game sheet and crayon or pencil. At the signal, players draw items containing their target sounds on their sacks. When time is up, players take turns naming three items at a time from their sacks. Give a point for each correct response. Award points for correct articulation only. The player with the most points wins.

For Objective 2: Distribute game sheets and crayons or pencils. Tell the players they are going to fill their sacks with items in the _____ category. The category may differ for each student, or you may change the category during the activity: "We have been drawing pictures of furniture. Now let's change to animals." Play the game as described for Objective 1.

For Objective 3: Distribute game sheets and crayons or pencils. Say, "You are going to fill your sacks with some interesting objects, but you will have to listen carefully to find out what they are." Make several incomplete statements, letting the players complete them orally.

Examples: I bounce a _____ .
I clap my _____ .
I love chocolate _____ .
"Meow!" says the _____ .

Then ask the players to draw all the items they have named on the sacks. When finished, players take turns telling what they can about the items. Can they recall what you said about each item?

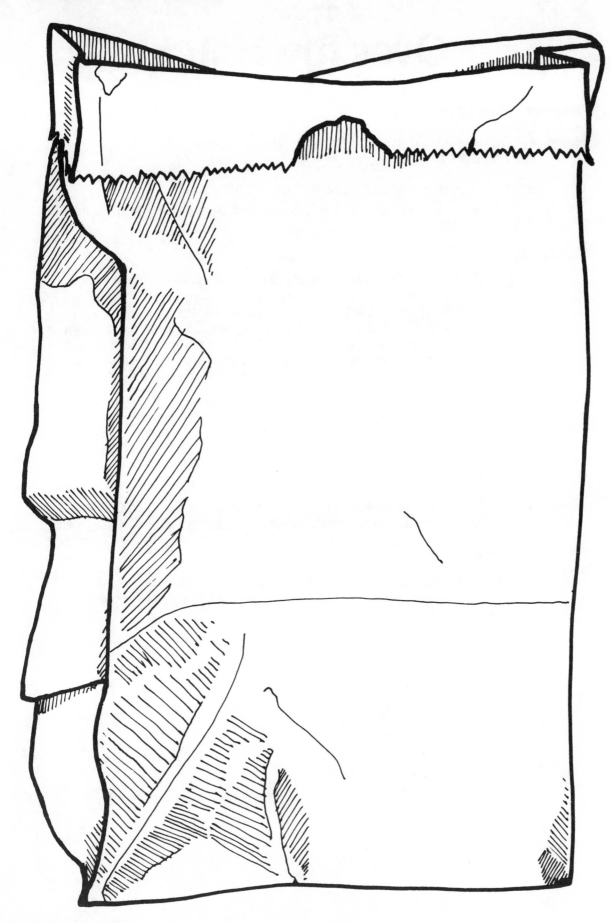

11
Over the Hill

Suggested Grade Level: K-3

Materials: Game sheet and marker for each player.
1-4 Spinner.

Objectives: 1. The student will correctly articulate a target sound.

           2. The student will use antonyms, synonyms, rhyming words, classification, etc.

Method of Play:

For Objective 1: Distribute the game sheets and markers. Players place their markers on *start*. Players take turns giving correct target sounds, spinning the 1-4 Spinner, and moving the indicated number of spaces. If the target sound is not correct, the player waits a turn and tries again. You may require that the target sound be articulated the same number of times as the number indicated on the spinner. The first player to climb over the hill to the *end* is the winner.

When working with the target sound in words, phrases, or sentences, write the stimulus words on the spaces before distributing the game sheets. Players take turns spinning the spinner, moving the indicated number of spaces, and responding to the stimulus in the space the marker lands on. If the response is incorrect, the player moves back one space and attempts the stimulus word in that space.

For Objective 2: Write stimulus words on the spaces on the game sheet and distribute the sheets. Markers are placed on *start*. The game is played as described for Objective 1. The first player to reach *end* is the winner.

When working with classification, have the players provide the number of items in a category corresponding to the number indicated on the spinner.

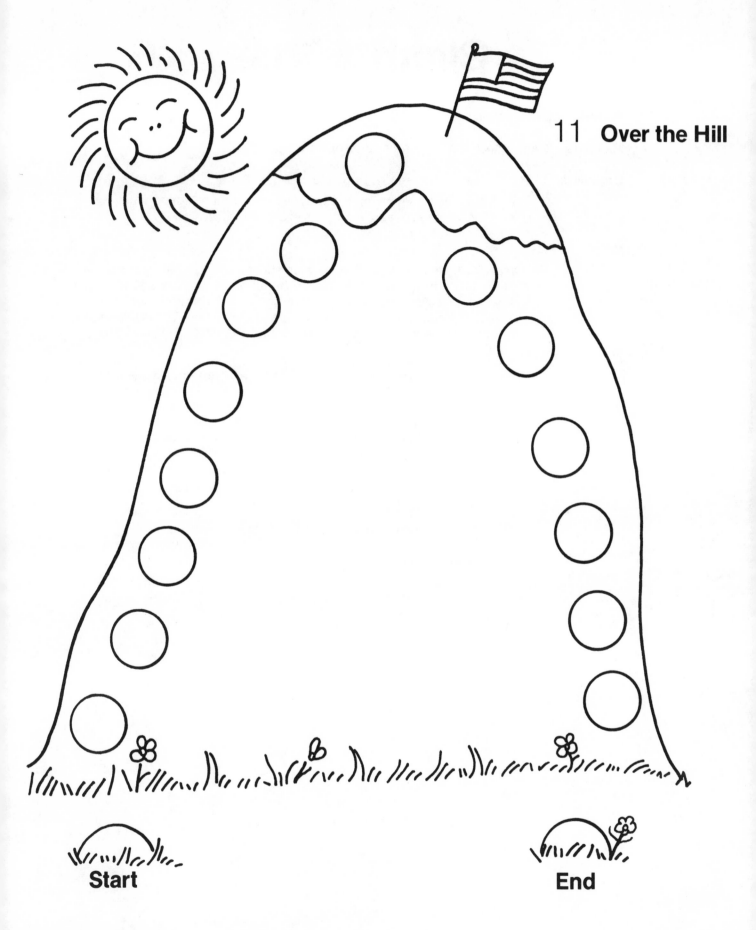

11 **Over the Hill**

Start

End

12
Climb a Tree

Suggested Grade Level: K-3

Materials: Game sheet and crayon or pencil for each player.

Objectives: 1. The student will correctly articulate a target sound.

2. The student will use rhyming concepts, will identify consonants or vowels, or will use vocabulary words in sentences.

Method of Play:

For Objective 1: Give each student a game sheet and a crayon or pencil. Players take turns repeating your production of a target sound in isolation or a word containing the target sound. If the response is correct, the player colors or marks a space on the tree. The object is to mark all the spaces, starting from the bottom and working to the top.

For Objective 2: Write stimulus words on the spaces. These may be words to be rhymed, words for consonant or vowel discrimination, or vocabulary words to be used in sentences. Give each player a game sheet and crayon or pencil. Starting at the bottom of the game sheet, players take turns responding to the stimuli. If a response is correct, the player colors or marks that space. In the next turn, the player moves to the next space, responds, and, if correct, continues to the next space. If a response is incorrect the player repeats that space on the next turn. The first player to reach the top is the winner.

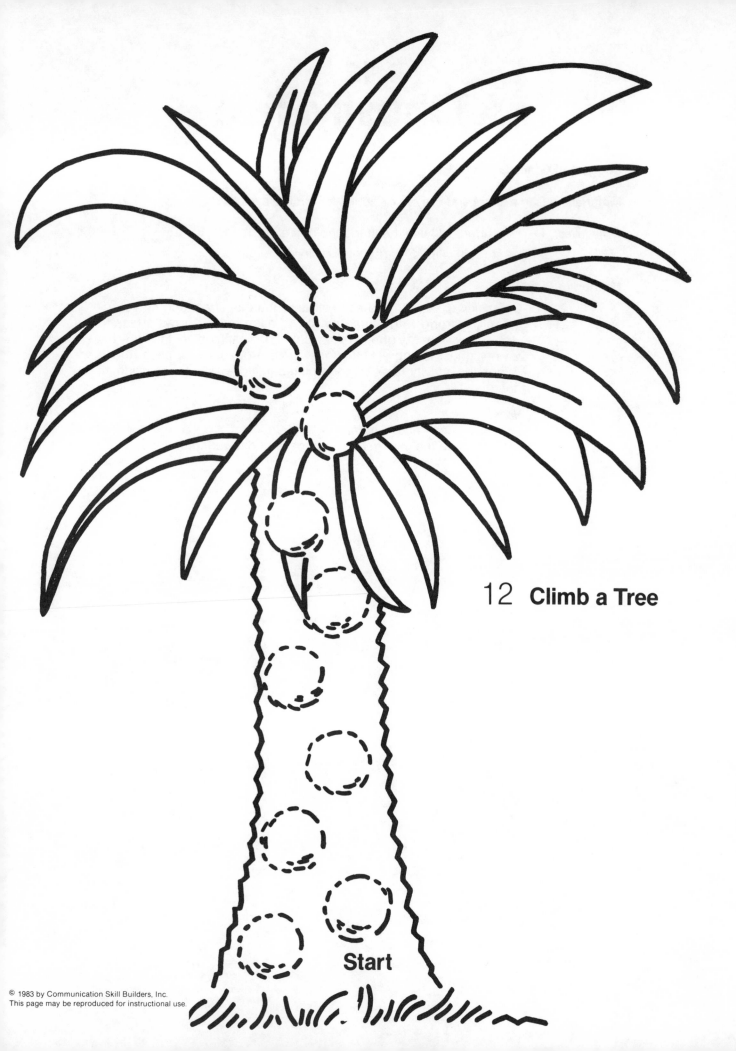

12 **Climb a Tree**

Start

13
A Ghostly Tale

Suggested Grade Level: K-3

Materials: Game sheet and crayon or pencil for each player.

Objectives: 1. The student will use the language of feelings.
            2. The student will use verbal expression.

Method of Play:

For Objectives 1 and 2: Give each student a game sheet and crayon or pencil. Starting with the *angry* ghost, each player draws a face to show how an angry ghost would look. Then each player tells why his or her ghost is angry. Follow the same procedure for each ghost. When the activity has been completed, tell or write stories using all the ghosts.

Possibilities:
Give each ghost a name.
Describe the experiences that caused different emotions.

14
Decorate the Tree

Suggested Grade Level: K-3

Materials: Game sheet and crayon or pencil for each player.

Objectives: 1. The student will discriminate a target sound.

2. The student will correctly articulate a target sound.

3. The student will use synonyms, antonyms, homonyms, rhyming words, classification, etc.

Method of Play:

For Objective 1: Give each player a game sheet and crayon or pencil. Tell the players to listen for the target sound. Say ten words with four of them containing the target sound. Each time the players hear the sound, they color or mark a space. The target sound may be changed for each round.

Example: In the first round, ask the players to listen for the **S** sound. Say ten words, four of which contain the **S** sound. Then ask the players to listen for the **TH** sound. Say another group of ten words, etc.

The object of the game is to color or mark all the ornaments.

For Objective 2: Distribute the game sheets and crayons or pencils. Provide oral stimuli in the form of words, phrases, or sentences that contain the target sound. Players take turns repeating a stimulus. If correct, the player decorates an ornament while the next player responds. If incorrect, the player tries again on the next turn.

For Objective 3: Write the selected stimuli on the game sheet, one per ornament. Distribute the game sheets and crayons or pencils. Players take turns selecting an ornament and providing an appropriate response. The object of the game is to decorate all the ornaments.

14 **Decorate the Tree**

15
Popcorn

Suggested Grade Level: K-3

Materials: Game sheet and crayon or pencil for each player.

Objectives: 1. The student will discriminate a target sound.

2. The student will correctly articulate a target sound.

3. The students will provide antonyms, synonyms, adjectives, rhyming words, correct verb tense, etc.

Method of Play:

For Objective 1: Distribute game sheets and crayons or pencils. Ask the players to color or mark a piece of popcorn when they hear the target sound. Players listen as you produce the target sound in syllables, words, phrases, or sentences. Players mark their game sheets only when they hear the correct production.

For Objective 2: Write stimulus words containing the target sound on the spaces. Distribute the game sheets and crayons or pencils. Players take turns selecting a piece of popcorn and articulating the sound, word, or phrase correctly. If correct, the player colors or marks that space. The player marking the most spaces is the winner.

For Objective 3: Write the stimuli on the spaces and distribute the game sheets and crayons or pencils. Players take turns selecting a piece of popcorn and providing an appropriate response to the stimulus. If correct, the student colors or marks that space. The student marking the most pieces of popcorn is the winner.

15 **Popcorn**

16
Flapjacks

Suggested Grade Level: K-3

Materials: Game sheets and crayon or pencil for each player.

Objectives: 1. The student will differentiate between similar stimuli.

2. The student will correctly produce a target sound.

3. The student will use antonyms, synonyms, adjectives, adverbs, etc.

Method of Play:

For Objective 1: Use this activity for discrimination tasks such as recognizing voiced and unvoiced sounds or correct and incorrect production of a target sound. Give each player a game sheet and a crayon or pencil. Ask the players to listen for the target sound and color a flapjack when the sound is recognized. Monitor each response and correct errors. The object is to color all the flapjacks.

For Objective 2: Write a word containing the target sound on each flapjack. Distribute the game sheets and crayons or pencils. Players take turns selecting a flapjack and articulating the stimulus word. For every correct response the player colors or marks that space. If the production is incorrect, the player is allowed another turn. The object of the game is to color or mark all the flapjacks.

For Objective 3: Write appropriate stimuli on the flapjacks and distribute the game sheets. Players take turns selecting a flapjack and responding to the stimulus. If the response is correct, that flapjack is colored or marked. The object is to mark all the flapjacks.

16 Flapjacks

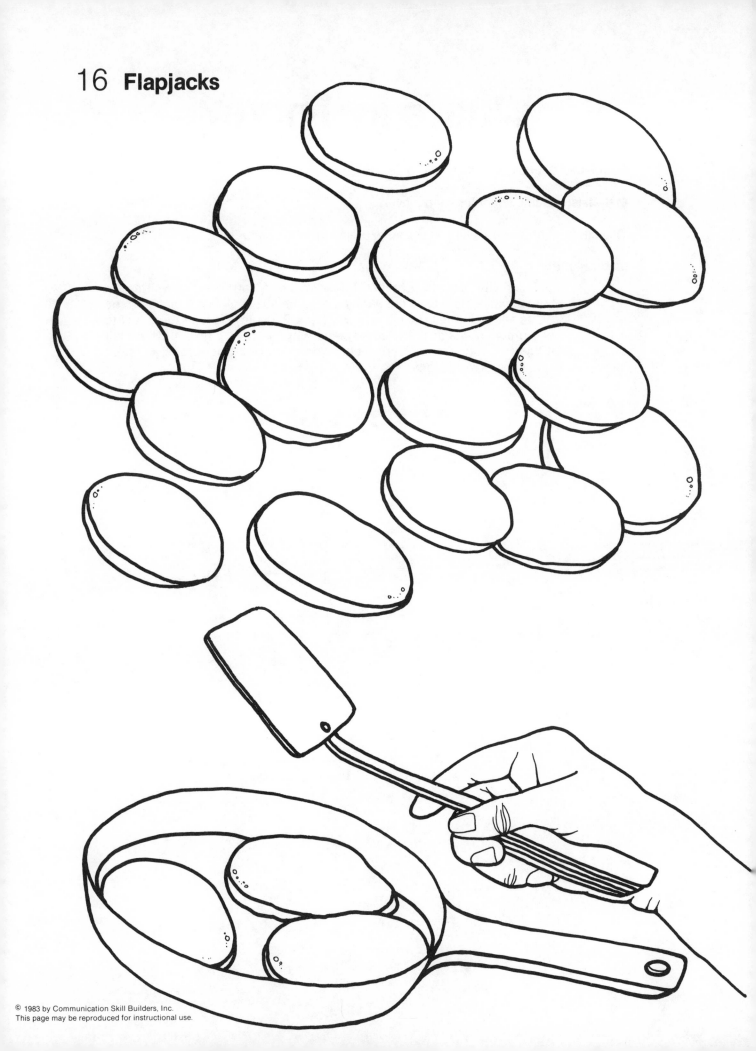

17
What's in There?

Suggested Grade Level: K-3

Materials: Game sheet for each player.

Objective: The student will use verbal expression.

Method of Play:

> This activity provides practice for articulation carryover as well as for verbal expression. Give each player a game sheet. Select a place on the game sheet and tell the players what it is. The players take turns telling what might be inside the selected place, why it is there, who could have left it there, and how the player feels upon finding it. Encourage as much verbalization as possible.

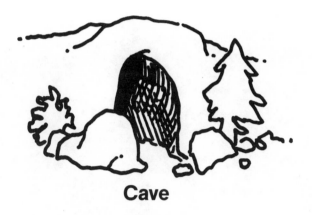

Cave

Haunted House

Treasure Chest

Hole in the Ground

Wallet

Shopping Bag

17 **What's in There?**

All the Games Kids Like
K-4

18
What Did They Say?

Suggested Grade Level: K-4

Materials: Game sheet and pencil for each player.

Objective: The student will use verbal expression.

Method of Play:

This activity provides practice for articulation carryover as well as for verbal expression. Give each player a game sheet and a pencil. Ask the players to think about what each character might be saying. Older players can write the words in the balloons beside each character. Younger players can tell you what the characters are saying so you can write it in. When all the balloons are filled in, discuss and compare the different ideas. Conversations between the characters may be made up by the players. They may enjoy writing playlets using these characters and the conversations discussed by the group.

18 **What Did They Say?**

19
Pussy Cat, Pussy Cat

Suggested Grade Level: K-4

Materials: Game sheet and pencil for each player.

Objectives: 1. The student will correctly articulate a target sound.
2. The student will identify feelings.

Method of Play:

For Objective 1: Write words containing the target sound between each cat's ears. Distribute the game sheets and pencils. Players take turns selecting a cat and articulating the word belonging to it. If the response is correct, the player draws a face on that cat. The object of the game is to draw faces on all the cats. When all the faces are completed, encourage the players to talk about their drawings using the target sounds correctly.

For Objective 2: Distribute the game sheets and pencils. Ask the players to draw specific faces on the cats.

Examples: Draw a sad cat.
Draw a cat that is furious.
Other stimuli: delighted, frightened, happy, frustrated, ill, upset, excited, worried.

Play continues until each cat has a face. Discuss and describe the faces for vocabulary reinforcement.

46

Pussy Cat, Pussy Cat

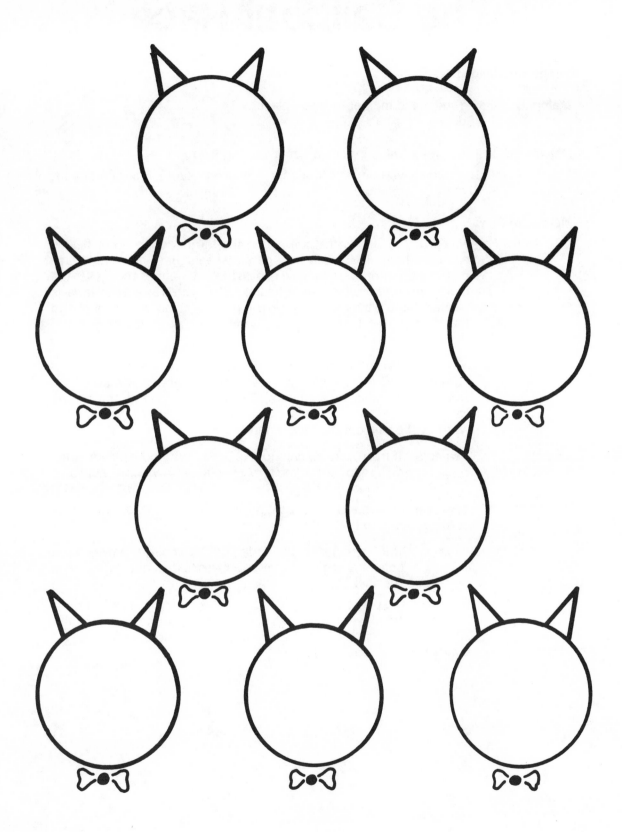

20
The Sailboat Race

Suggested Grade Level: K-4

Materials: Game sheet and marker for each player.
1-4 Spinner.

Objectives: 1. The student will correctly articulate a target sound.

2. The student will use parts of speech, antonyms, synonyms, homonyms, rhyming words, etc.

Method of Play:

For Objective 1: Write words containing the target sound on or beside each sailboat. Distribute the game sheets and markers. Place markers on *start*. The first player spins the 1-4 Spinner and moves the indicated number of spaces, articulating the words as each sailboat is passed. If the player makes an error, play stops on that sailboat and the next player takes a turn. The first player to reach *finish* is the winner.

For Objective 2: Write a stimulus word on or beside each sailboat. Distribute the game sheets and markers. Players place their markers on *start*. Players take turns spinning the 1-4 Spinner and moving the indicated number of sailboats. A player responds to the stimulus word by the sailboat the marker lands on.

Example: If the response category is *adjectives* and a player lands on a sailboat marked *bird,* the player provides an adjective that describes a bird.

A player may be required to provide a number of adjectives corresponding to the number indicated by the spinner.

Example: If the spinner arrow landed on 3, the player moves three spaces and gives three adjectives to describe the word by the sailboat.

If correct, the player remains on that sailboat until the next turn. If incorrect, the player moves back one sailboat and responds to the stimulus for that sailboat. The object of the game is to be the first player to reach *finish.*

20 **The Sailboat Race**

Start

Finish

No wind.
Miss turn.

High wind.
Go fast.

Have
advantage.
Take
extra
turn.

Ahead
1 space.

21
The Secret Window

Suggested Grade Level: K-4

Materials: Game sheet and pencil for each player.

Objectives: 1. The student will correctly articulate a target sound.

2. The student will use verbal expression.

3. The student will attend to verbalization.

Method of Play:

For Objective 1: Distribute the game sheets and pencils. Assign target sounds according to players' individual needs. A player names an object that might be seen in the Secret Window. The object must contain the assigned target sound. If the target sound is articulated correctly, the player draws the object on the game sheet while the next player takes a turn.

For Objective 2: Give each player a game sheet and pencil. Ask the first player to tell a short story about something that might be seen through the Secret Window. After telling a story, the player draws the object on the game sheet. To encourage the beginning of a story, you may have to elicit some single-word responses by asking questions.

Examples: What would you see if you peeked through the window?
What is it doing there?
Who put it there?
What is going to happen?

For Objective 3: Write words following a theme on the window on each game sheet.

Examples: monster, queen, jewels, prince, cave, forest, necklace, horse, castle.

Tell the players that they must listen to each other carefully. The first player selects a word and uses it in a sentence that serves to begin a story. The next player selects another word and uses it in a sentence that relates to the first sentence. As the players select words and compose sentences, a story will emerge. After all the words are used, ask one player to retell the story or to summarize it. The players may be asked questions about the story.

21 **The Secret Window**

All the Games Kids Like
K-6

22
Bunch of Grapes

Suggested Grade Level: K-6

Materials: Game sheet and pencil or crayon for each player.

Objectives: 1. The student will correctly articulate a target sound.

   2. The student will use synonyms, antonyms, homonyms, correct verb tense, pronouns, etc.

Method of Play:

For Objective 1: Write words containing the target sound on the grapes. Distribute the game sheets and pencils or crayons. Players take turns selecting a grape and saying the stimulus word correctly or using it in a sentence. If the response is correct, the player marks or colors the grape. The player marking the most grapes is the winner.

Variation:
Older players may write the words themselves while being timed. When time is up, the players take turns saying the words they have written and marking each one off as it is articulated correctly. A point can be awarded for each word spoken and written correctly. The player with the most points is the winner.

For Objective 2: Write the stimulus words on the grapes. Distribute the game sheets and crayons or pencils. A player selects a grape and gives the required response. If correct, the player marks or colors the grape. The player marking the most grapes is the winner.

Variation:
Give the stimuli orally. The players respond orally and then write their correct responses on the game sheets.

22 **Bunch of Grapes**

23
What's in the Purse?

Suggested Grade Level: K-6

Materials: Game sheet and crayons for each player.

Objectives: 1. The student will correctly articulate a target sound.

2. The student will use verbal expression.

3. The student will improve auditory reception.

Method of Play:

For Objective 1: Distribute the game sheets and crayons. Ask the players to name objects that might be found in a purse. The name of each object must contain the target sound. Set a time limit on the game. Each player in turn names an object. If the target sound is articulated correctly, the player draws a picture of the item on the purse. The player with the most objects on the purse when time is up is the winner.

For Objective 2: Give the players game sheets and crayons. Players take turns naming items that might be found in a purse, describing them, and telling how they are used. If correct, the player draws the item on the purse. The object of the game is to draw as many items as will fit on the purse.

For Objective 3: Give each player a game sheet and crayons. Ask them to think of an item they might find in a purse but not to reveal what it is. The first player gives a clue about an item and the other players try to guess what the item is. Clues continue until someone guesses correctly. The player who gave the clues draws that item on the purse. Players take turns giving clues and guessing until there is no more room on the purse or until time is up.

56

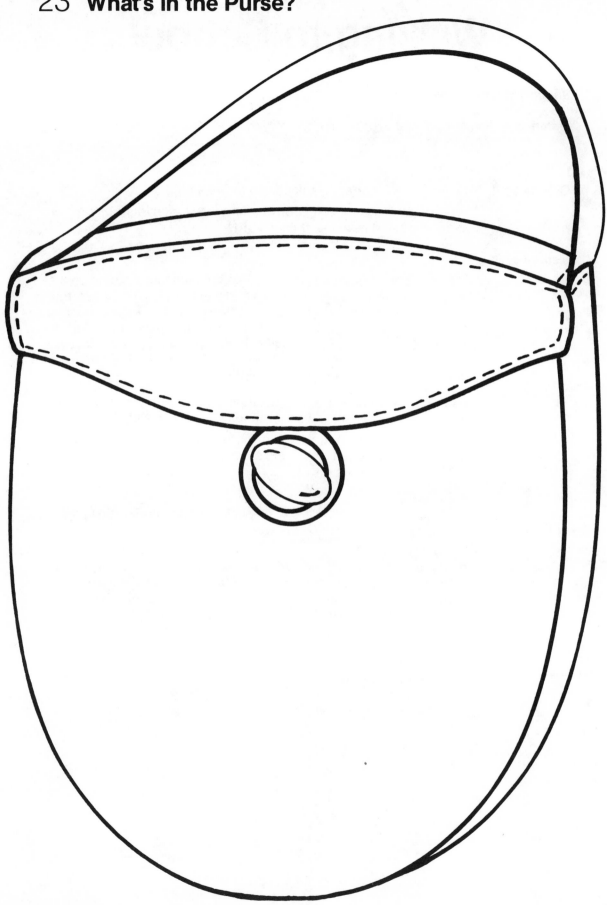

24
Walking to School

Suggested Grade Level: K-6

Materials: Game sheet and marker for each player.
1-4 Spinner.

Objectives: 1. The student will correctly articulate a target sound.

2. The student will use rhyming words, antonyms, synonyms, homonyms, classification and new vocabulary words.

Method of Play:

For Objective 1: Write stimulus words containing the target sound on the spaces. Distribute the game sheets and markers. Tell the players that they are going to follow the path from *home* to *school* and practice their target sounds on the way. Players in turn place a marker on *home,* spin the 1-4 Spinner, and move the marker the indicated number of spaces. The player then says the word on the space the marker landed on the indicated number of times.

Example: If the spinner arrow stops at 4, the player moves four spaces and says the stimulus word correctly four times.

The player records a point for each correct production on that space. The game ends when all players are at *school.* Points are totaled to determine the winner.

Variation:

The game does not have to be played for points. The first player to reach *school* can be the winner.

For Objective 2: Write the stimulus words on the spaces and distribute the game sheets and markers. All the markers are placed on *home.* Players take turns spinning the 1-4 Spinner, moving the marker the indicated number of spaces, and responding to the stimulus word on the final space. If the task has several responses to a single stimulus word, such as in classification, the player might be asked to provide the number of responses corresponding to the number indicated by the spinner. A point could be awarded for each correct response and the player with the most points is the winner. If the task can have only one response, the player provides that single response and the first player to reach *school* is the winner.

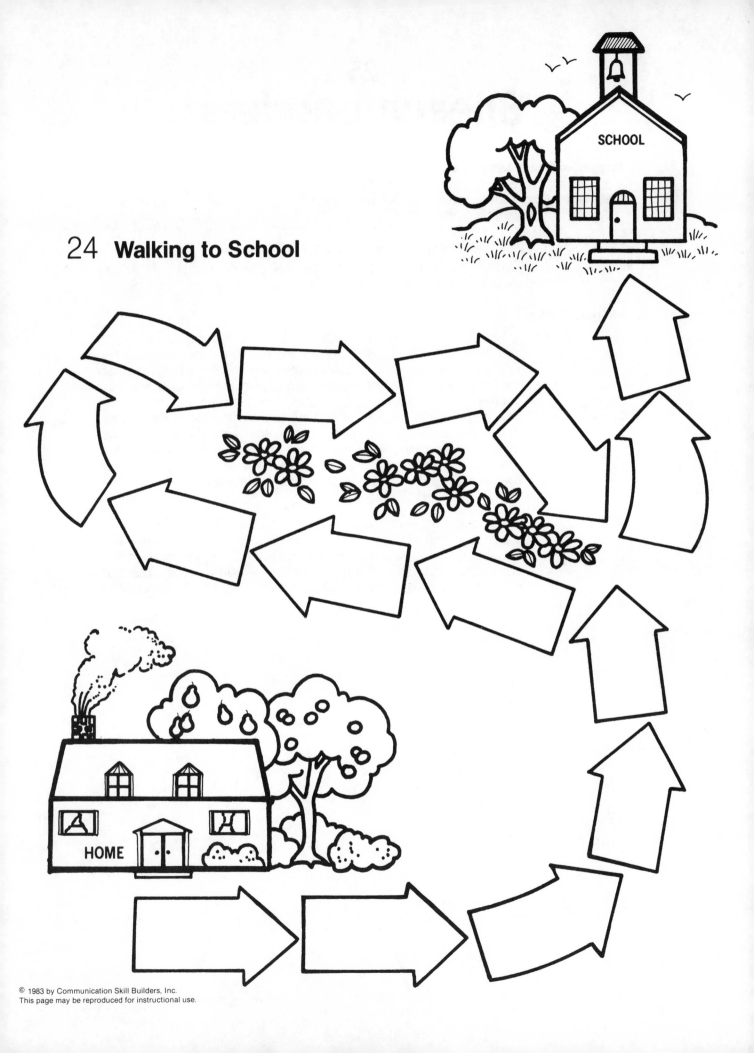

24 **Walking to School**

25
Speech Ladders

Suggested Grade Level: K-6

Materials: Game sheet and marker for each player.
1-4 Spinner.

Objectives: 1. The student will correctly articulate a target sound.

2. The student will use antonyms, synonyms, homonyms, plurals, adjectives, adverbs, etc.

Method of Play:

For Objective 1: Write stimulus words containing the target sound on the spaces. Distribute the game sheets and markers. Place the markers on *start.* Players take turns spinning the 1-4 Spinner, moving a marker the indicated number of spaces, and saying the stimulus word as each space is crossed. When a marker lands on a space at the bottom of a ladder, the player moves it to the space at the top of the ladder. The player says the stimulus word on that space and leaves the marker there until the next turn. Markers are not moved down a ladder unless a more difficult game is desired. If the response is incorrect, the marker remains on the space where the error was made. The winner is the first to reach *end.*

For Objective 2: Write stimulus words on the spaces. Distribute the game sheets and markers. Play this game as described for Objective 1, but the stimuli differ. Players may respond only to the stimuli on the spaces they land on rather than to all passed on the path. The first player to reach *end* is the winner.

25 Speech Ladders

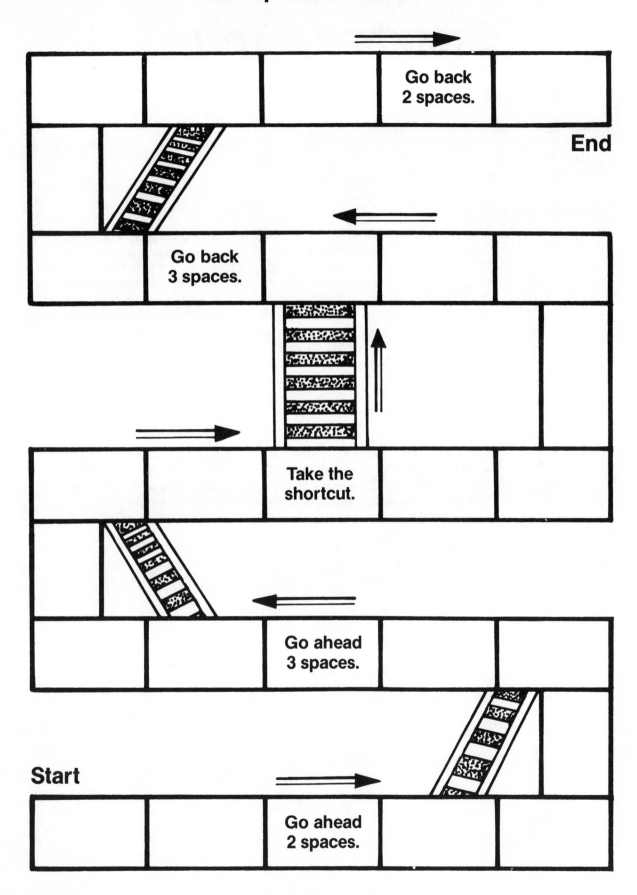

26
Grandma's Trunk

Suggested Grade Level: K-6

Materials: Game sheet and crayon or pencil for each player.

Objectives: 1. The student will correctly articulate a target sound.
2. The student will use classification.

Method of Play:

For Objective 1: Write stimulus words containing the target sound on each space on the key. Distribute the game sheets and crayons or pencils. Tell the players that Grandma kept this trunk in her attic for many years. The only way to open it is to correctly say the words written on the key. A player says one of the words on the key. If correct, the player marks off that space and draws an object containing the target sound on the trunk. Then the next player takes a turn. When all the words on the key have been marked, players take turns telling what they drew on their trunks. These words should be articulated correctly. A point may be awarded for each correct production. These objects make excellent topics for discussion and carryover of a target sound.

For Objective 2: Write the name of a category on each space on the key. Distribute the game sheets and crayons or pencils. Tell players that they can open the trunk only if they provide items in each category. The first player selects a space on the key and names an item in that category. If correct, the player draws the item or writes its name on the trunk while the next player takes a turn, using the same space on the key. When no more responses can be provided for that category, the next space is selected and the activity continues. When all the spaces on the key have been used, the player with the most items in the trunk is the winner.

26 Grandma's Trunk

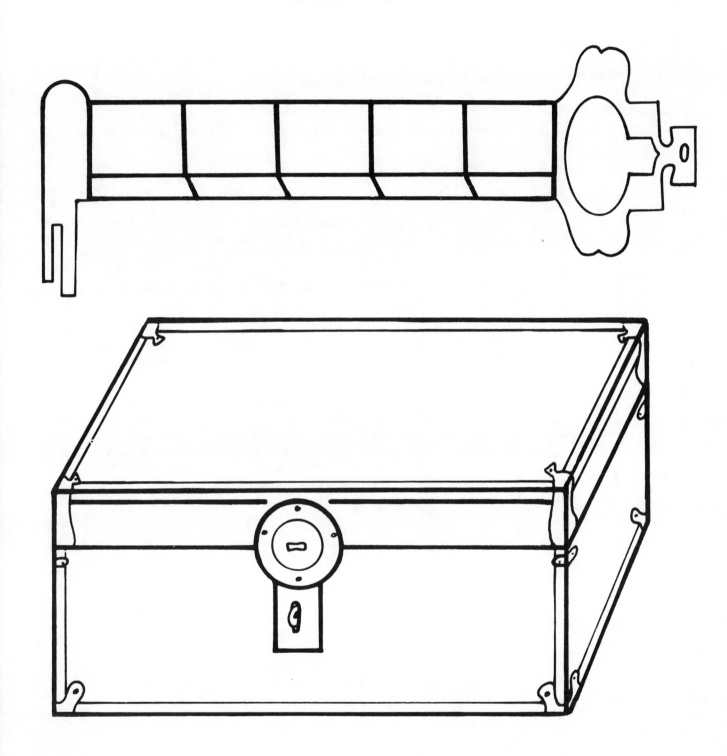

27
Flower Game

Suggested Grade Level: K-6

Materials: Game sheet and crayons for each player.

Objectives: 1. The student will correctly articulate a target sound.
 2. The student will use antonyms, synonyms, rhyming words, homonyms, etc.
 3. The student will use classification.

Method of Play:

For Objective 1: Write a stimulus word containing the target sound on each petal of the flower. Distribute the game sheets and crayons. Players take turns selecting a petal and articulating the stimulus word correctly or using it in a sentence, as instructed. If correct, the player colors the petal. The object of the game is to color all the petals on the flower.

For Objective 2: Write a stimulus word on each petal of the flower. Distribute the game sheets and crayons. The stimuli may vary from one player to the next, depending upon individual need. The game is played as described for Objective 1.

For Objective 3: Write a category on each petal of the flower. Distribute the game sheets and crayons. Players take turns selecting a petal and naming as many items in the category on that petal as possible. The player records the number of correct responses on the selected petal. When the game sheets are completed, the responses on each are totaled. The player with the highest number is the winner.

28
To the Zoo

Suggested Grade Level: K-6

Materials: Game sheet and pencil for each player.
1-4 Spinner.

Objectives: 1. The student will use classification, specifically animals.

              2. The student will improve auditory reception.

              3. The student will use description.

Method of Play:

For Objective 1: Distribute the game sheets and pencils. Tell the players that they are going on a trip to the zoo. Players take turns spinning the 1-4 Spinner, naming the corresponding number of animals that might be found at the zoo, and drawing a picture of each animal or writing their names on the signs—one picture or name to a sign.

> *Example:* If the spinner arrow stops at 2, the player names two animals, such as a monkey and a zebra. On the first sign on the game sheet, the player draws a monkey and on the next sign the same player draws a zebra. It is then the next player's turn.

An animal may not be named twice. Players must listen and remember which animals have been named. The first player to arrive at the zoo is the winner.

For Objective 2: Write a series of riddles or questions according to the players' age levels and abilities. Distribute the game sheets and pencils. Tell the players they are going on a trip to the zoo. Ask them riddles or questions about the animals in the zoo.

> *Examples:* What animal has black and white stripes?
> I am thinking of an animal with a very long neck.

If the response is correct, the player spins the spinner and moves the number of spaces indicated. The first student to reach the zoo wins.

For Objective 3: Write the name of an animal on each sign on the game sheet. Distribute the game sheets and pencils. The first player spins the 1-4 Spinner, moves the indicated number of spaces, and describes the animal written on that space. If the description is acceptable, the player receives a point. After all players complete the path, the one with the most points is the winner.

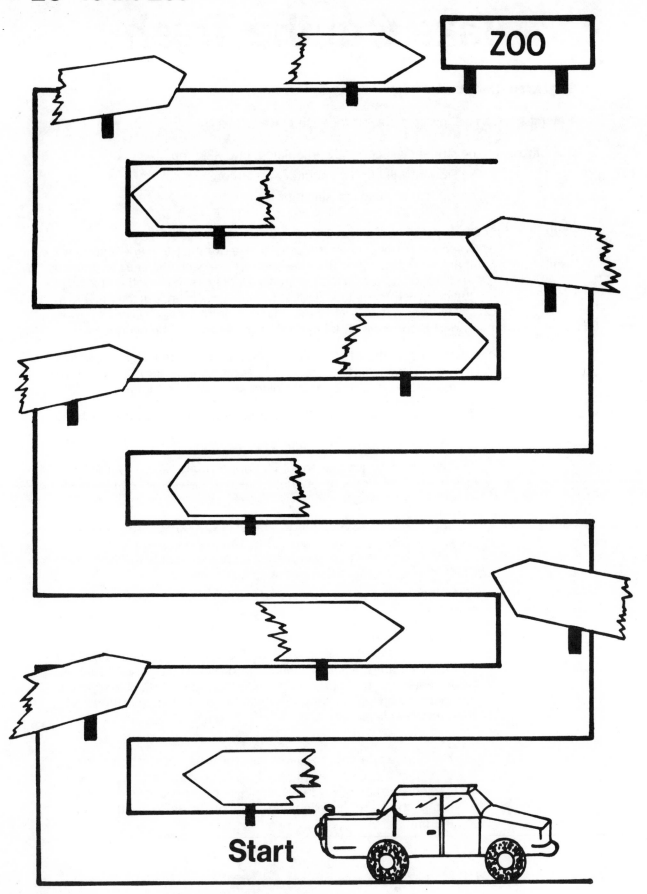

ZOO

Start

29
Take Out the Trash

Suggested Grade Level: K-6

Materials: Game sheet and crayon for each player.

Objectives: 1. The student will correctly articulate a target sound.
2. The student will improve auditory reception.
3. The student will use classification.

Method of Play:

For Objective 1: Tell players they are to take out the trash and it contains many objects using their target sound. Give each player a game sheet and crayon. Establish a time limit. Ask players to draw the objects in the trash within the time limit. When the time is up, ask the players to tell what is in their trash cans. Award a point for each correct target-sound production. Total the points to determine the winner.

For Objective 2: Distribute the game sheets and crayons. Tell the players they are going to fill their trash cans. Provide oral stimuli as questions or riddles. Players draw each object they are able to name.

Examples: 1. I am thinking of something you wear on your head when it rains.
2. You ride this and it has two wheels.

Responses may vary but should be appropriate. Once a stimulus is given and the drawing of that object is complete, compare the responses in a discussion.

Example: Both bicycle and motorcycle are correct responses for Example 2, above. Ask the players who gave those answers to compare their responses, citing the similarities and differences of the vehicles.

The object of the game is to fill the trash can with as many objects as possible.

For Objective 3: Give each player a game sheet and a crayon. Tell the players they will be filling their trash cans with objects in the same category. Establish a time limit and announce a category. At a signal, players begin to draw objects on their trash cans that belong in the category. When time is up, ask players to tell what objects they put in their trash cans.

Variation:
Announce a category. Players take turns naming an object in that category. If correct, the player draws the object on the trash can. Change the category after each player has responded or when no more objects can be named. The object is to fill the can to the brim.

Take Out the Trash

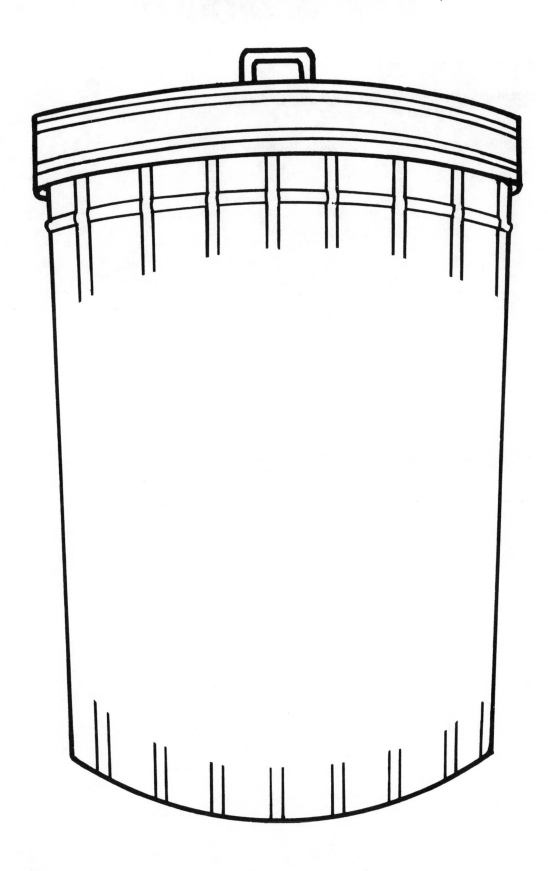

30
Eek! A Mouse!

Suggested Grade Level: K-6

Materials: Game sheet and marker for each player.
Plus and Minus Spinner.

Objective: The student will correctly articulate a target sound.

Method of Play:

If the spinner arrow stops at a number that has the *plus* symbol, the player moves the marker *forward* the number of spaces designated. If the spinner arrow stops at a number that has a *minus* symbol, the marker is moved *backward* that number of spaces. Write the stimuli containing the target sound beside the pieces of cheese. Distribute the game sheets and markers. Players take turns spinning the Plus and Minus Spinner, moving their markers from space 1 to space 12, and saying each of the stimulus words passed. The first student to reach the last piece of cheese is the winner.

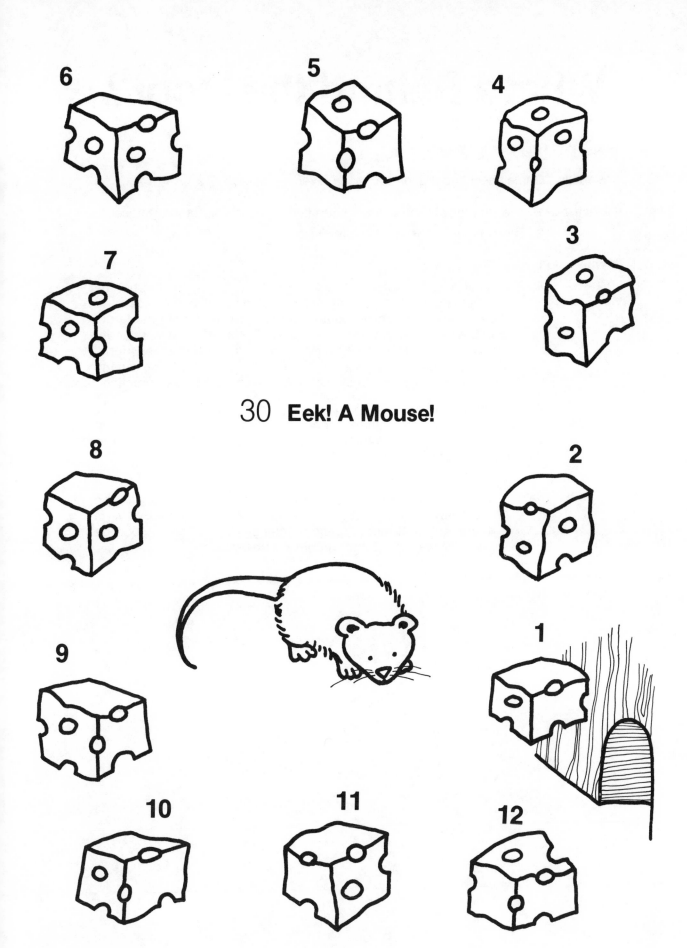

30 **Eek! A Mouse!**

31
What's Behind the Door?

Suggested Grade Level: K-6

Materials: Game sheet and crayon for each player.

Objectives: 1. The student will use a target sound correctly in spontaneous speech.
2. The student will use verbal expression.

Method of Play:

For Objective 1: Give each player a game sheet and crayon. Instruct the players to draw a picture of an object that might be behind the door. The name of each object behind the door must contain the target sound. When drawings are complete, each player tells a story about the object behind the door, carefully articulating the target sound. When a player articulates a word incorrectly, write that word on the game sheet. The player may then take it home for further practice.

For Objective 2: Distribute the game sheets and crayons. Tell the players to draw something they think might be hidden behind the door. When all the drawings are complete, the players take turns telling stories about the objects that are hidden behind the door.

Variation:
Let older players pretend to be reporters covering a story for the local newspaper. Ask them to describe the object and tell why it is there and what the outcome of their stories will be. Encourage other players to ask the "reporter" questions.

What's Behind the Door?

All the Games Kids Like
K-8

32
Picking Pockets

Suggested Grade Level: K-8

Materials: Game sheet and pencil for each player.

Objectives: 1. The student will correctly articulate a target sound.
  2. The student will use verbal expression.
  3. The student will improve auditory sequential memory.

Method of Play:

For Objective 1: Give each student a game sheet and pencil. Specify if you want the response in words or sentences. A player selects a pocket and tells what it might contain in a word or sentence that contains the target sound. The player draws a picture of that object on the selected pocket. Play continues until all pockets have pictures.

Variation:

Before distributing the game sheets, write the name of an object containing the target sound under each pocket. A player selects a pocket, says the stimulus word correctly, and draws the object on the pocket.

For Objective 2: Give each student a game sheet and pencil. Players take turns telling what object might be in a specific pocket, who put it there and why, and what could be done with it. Then ask the players to name some related objects.

Example: A screwdriver is used by a carpenter who put it in the pocket so it couldn't be lost. It is used for building a house. Other tools used by a carpenter are a hammer, a wrench, and pliers.

For Objective 3: Distribute game sheets and pencils. The first player selects a pocket and names something that might be in that pocket. The second player selects a pocket and names something that might be in it, adding the object the first player named. The third player names an object to be in another pocket and adds the objects named by the other two players. The list builds in this way until all pockets have been used. Players might be asked to draw the objects in the respective pockets. When a player forgets the order of the objects, ask the other players to provide hints.

32 **Picking Pockets**

All the Games Kids Like
1-4

33
Bruno's Night Out

Suggested Grade Level: 1-4

Materials: Game sheet and marker for each player.
1-4 Spinner.

Objectives: 1. The student will correctly articulate a target sound.

2. The student will complete sentences.

Method of Play:

For Objective 1: Write stimulus words containing the target sound on the game sheet and provide each player with a game sheet and marker. Markers are place on *start.* A player spins the 1-4 Spinner and moves the indicated number of spaces. When landing on a space, the player must articulate the stimulus word the number of times indicated by the spinner or use it in a sentence. If correct, the player remains on that space. If incorrect, the player moves back one space and articulates the word on that space. The first student to reach the doghouse is the winner.

For Objective 2: Write incomplete sentences on each space on the game sheet. Distribute the sheets and markers. Play the game as described for Objective 1.

Variation:
Incomplete sentences may be used to elicit syntactical elements, adjectives, adverbs, antonyms, synonyms, classification, or another desired response.

33 **Bruno's Night Out**

Start

**Find bone.
Take extra turn.**

**Stop to sniff.
Go back 2 spaces.**

**Chase a cat.
Miss a turn.**

BRUNO

34
It Does What?

Suggested Grade Level: 1-4

Materials: Game sheet and marker for each player.

Objectives: 1. The student will use verbal expression.
                 2. The student will use adjectives.

Method of Play:

For Objective 1: Give each player a game sheet and a marker. The markers are placed on *start.* The first player moves a marker one space and tells something that can be done with the object in that space or something that the object can do.

Examples: A light bulb belongs in a lamp and it makes light.
Light bulbs help us see in the dark.

A point is awarded for each correct response. A player unable to give an acceptable response does not score the point but does continue on the path. Each player has a chance for each space. The game ends when all the players have reached *end.* Total the points to determine the winner.

For Objective 2: Give each player a game sheet and marker. Play proceeds as described for Objective 1 but the task differs. The first player moves the marker to a space and provides at least one adjective to describe the object on that space. A point is awarded for each appropriate response. At the end of the game, the player with the most points is the winner.

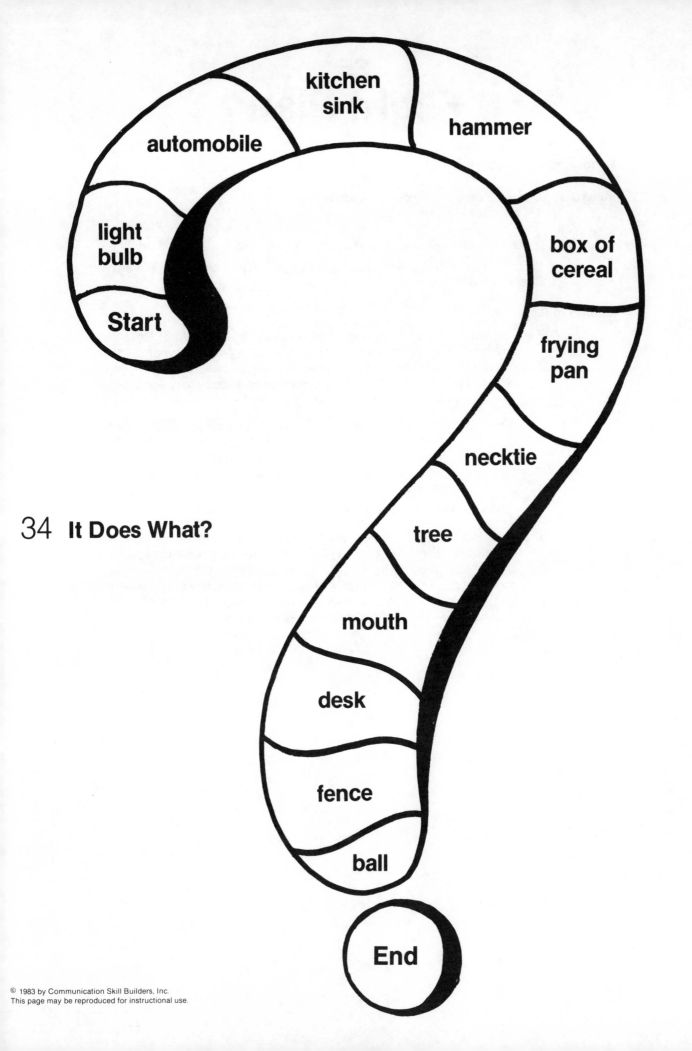

kitchen
sink

automobile

hammer

light
bulb

box of
cereal

Start

frying
pan

necktie

34 It Does What?

tree

mouth

desk

fence

ball

End

35
Flight Plan

Suggested Grade Level: 1-4

Materials: Game sheet and marker for each player.
1-4 Spinner.

Objectives: 1. The student will correctly articulate a target sound in isolation.

2. The student will correctly articulate a target sound in a word or sentence.

Method of Play:

For Objective 1: Give each player a game sheet and marker. The markers are placed on *start.* The first player spins the 1-4 Spinner and articulates the target sound the number of times indicated by the spinner arrow. The player then moves the marker one space for each time the target sound was produced correctly.

Example: The spinner arrow stops on 4. The player articulates the target sound four times, making an error the third time. The player then moves the marker three spaces instead of four, because the target sound was correctly articulated three out of the four attempts.

The first player to reach the airplane is the winner.

For Objective 2: Write stimulus words on the spaces. Distribute the game sheets and markers. The first player spins the spinner and moves the indicated number of spaces. The player may be required to respond to each space passed. When arriving on a space, the player says the stimulus word a given number of times or uses it in a sentence. The first player to reach the airplane wins the game.

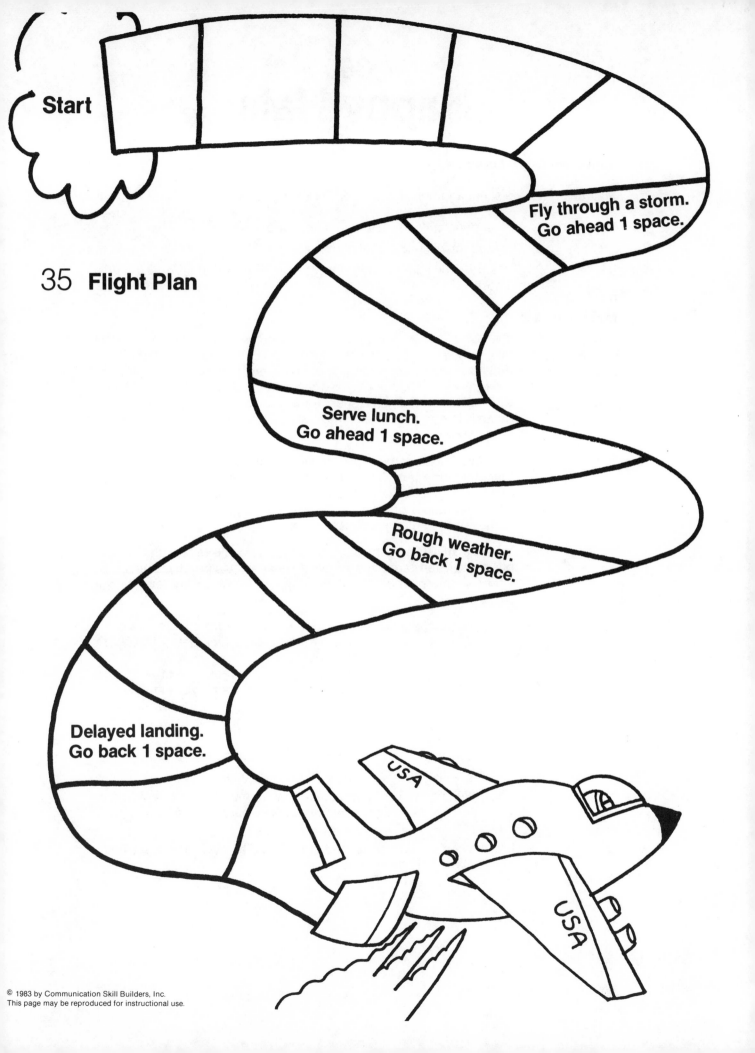

Start

35 **Flight Plan**

Fly through a storm.
Go ahead 1 space.

Serve lunch.
Go ahead 1 space.

Rough weather.
Go back 1 space.

Delayed landing.
Go back 1 space.

USA

USA

36
Happy Hats

Suggested Grade Level: 1-4

Materials: Game sheet and pencil or crayon for each player.

Objectives: 1. The student will correctly articulate a target sound.

2. The student will use verbal expression.

3. The student will improve auditory reception and auditory sequential memory.

Method of Play:

For Objective 1: Distribute the game sheets and pencils or crayons. Players take turns selecting a hat and describing the person who might wear that hat—the person's job, appearance, etc. If no errors are made on the target sounds, the player draws a face beneath the hat. Record error words on the game sheet for further practice. The object of the game is to complete the game sheet without making an error on the target sound.

For Objective 2: The game is played as described for Objective 1 except that other criteria are substituted for the target sound. Criteria might include using specific pronouns, verb tenses, descriptive language, whole sentences of a certain length, etc. Players draw faces on their game sheets if their responses meet the stated criteria.

For Objective 3: Distribute the game sheets and pencils or crayons. Tell the players to listen carefully so they can hear what to do. Give directions, either simple or multiple, depending upon the ability level of the players.

Examples: Simple Directions: Draw a face under the clown's hat. Draw a happy face below the chef's hat.

Multiple Directions: Draw a happy face under the clown's hat and then touch your knee. Draw a baby under the bonnet, give the baby a bottle, and tell what a baby would do.

Variation:
This activity can also use riddles as stimuli.

Example: I am thinking of someone who marches in a parade and leads a band. Can you find the hat? Draw a serious face below it.

Players find the proper hat and draw a face below it. The game ends when all the hats have faces.

36 Happy Hats

All the Games Kids Like
1-6

37
Haunted Mansion

Suggested Grade Level: 1-6

Materials: Game sheet and marker for each player.
1-4 Spinner.

Objective: The student will improve auditory sequential memory.

Method of Play

Give each student a game sheet and marker. Place all markers on *start*. The first player spins the 1-4 Spinner and moves the indicated number of spaces. The directions printed in that space are followed as stated. The next player spins the spinner and moves the marker as indicated. This player then repeats the first player's task and follows the directions given in the space where the second marker is. The third player spins, moves the marker, performs the tasks of the first and second players, and adds the one stated on the space where the third marker is. When there are so many tasks that the players cannot remember their sequence, play is discontinued or the game is started again. The player who can recall the most tasks is declared the winner.

Start

Touch your toes.

Cough.

Cover your face.

Clap your hands.

Smile.

Blink your eyes.

Say your name.

Tap the table.

37 **Haunted Mansion**

Put your hands behind you.

Whistle a tune.

Tap your foot.

Scratch your nose.

Sneeze.

Cover your ears.

Yawn.

Shake your head.

Clear your throat.

38
Footprints

Suggested Grade Level: 1-6

Materials: Game sheet and marker for each player.
1-4 Spinner.

Objectives: 1. The student will correctly articulate a target sound.

2. The student will use classification.

Method of Play

For Objective 1: Write stimulus words containing the target sound on the footprints. Distribute the game sheets and markers. Place the markers on *start.* The first player spins the 1-4 Spinner and moves the indicated number of spaces. The player may be required to do one of the following:

Move the marker to the designated space and say that word once.
Say the word a given number of times.
Use the word in a sentence.
Say each word as it is passed.

A correct response allows the player to remain on that space or to move forward. With an incorrect response, the player goes back one space. The first player to reach *end* is the winner.

For Objective 2: Write a category on each footprint. Distribute the game sheets and markers. All the markers are placed on *start.* For this objective, ignore the instructions beside the footprints. The first player moves the marker to the first footprint and spins the spinner. The number indicated by the spinner arrow is the number of responses the player must give for the category on the first footprint. The number of correct responses is recorded on the footprint. The next player responds to the same stimulus without duplicating the responses of the first player. When all players have arrived at *end,* the player with the most points is the winner.

Variation:

Players move the number of spaces indicated by the spinner arrow and also use that number to determine the number of responses to the stimulus word.

**A cool brook.
Go ahead 1.**

Start

**Stub your toe.
Go back 1.**

**Ouch! A rock!
Go back 1.**

End

**Walk through
mud. Go
ahead 1.**

39
Trail to the Castle

Suggested Grade Level: 1-6

Materials: Game sheet and marker for each player.
1-4 Spinner.

Objectives: 1. The student will correctly articulate a target sound.

2. The student will use adjectives, adverbs, antonyms, synonyms, etc.

Method of Play

For Objective 1: Write stimulus words containing the target sound on the spaces. Distribute the game sheets and markers. Players place their markers on *start.* Players take turns spinning the 1-4 Spinner, moving the indicated number of spaces, and saying each of the stimulus words as they are passed. If a response is incorrect, the player stops on that space.

Example: The spinner arrow points to 3. The player moves one space and says the word on that space correctly. On the second space, the player's response is incorrect. The player must stop on that space and wait for another turn to spin again. If all the responses are correct, the player stops on the third space.

The first player to reach the castle is the winner.

For Objective 2: Write stimulus words on the spaces. Distribute the game sheets and markers. Players place their markers on *start.* The first player spins the 1-4 Spinner and moves the indicated number of spaces, responding to the stimulus word on the final space. If correct, the marker remains on that space. If incorrect, the player moves back one space and responds to the stimulus word in that space. The object of the game is to be the first player to arrive at the castle.

Castle

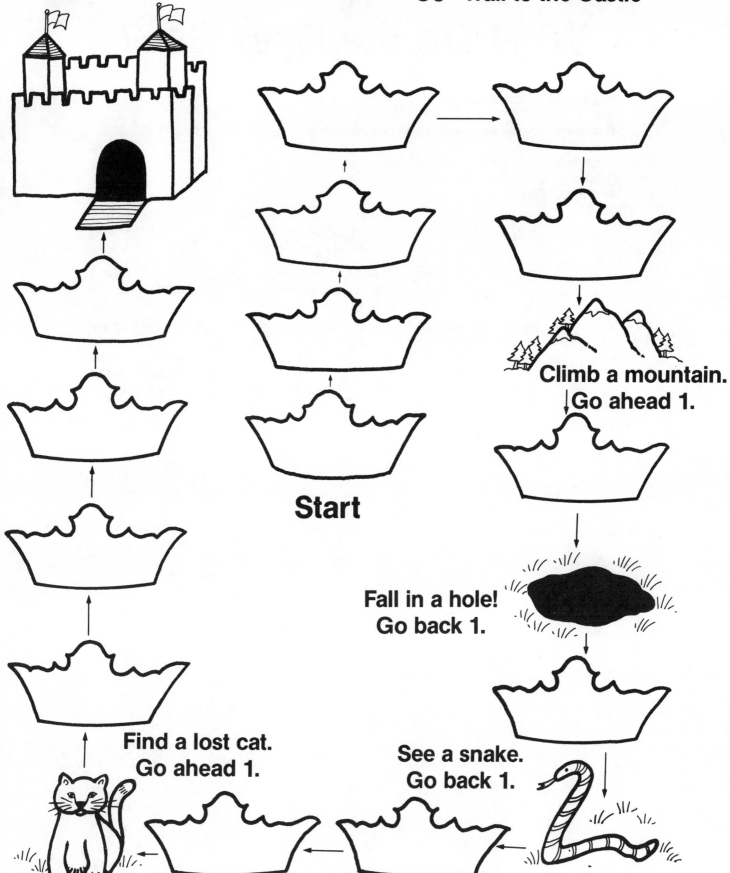

Climb a mountain.
Go ahead 1.

Start

Fall in a hole!
Go back 1.

Find a lost cat.
Go ahead 1.

See a snake.
Go back 1.

40
What Do the Eyes See?

Suggested Grade Level: 1-6

Materials: Game sheet and crayon for each player.

Objective: The student will use verbal expression.

Method of Play

Give each student a game sheet and crayon. The first player selects a pair of eyes and tells who or what the eyes could be looking at. Each player in turn responds to the same pair of eyes and compares ideas.

Example: The first player says the eyes in the A box are looking at a ghost. The second player disagrees and says they are watching a spy.

Discuss the reasons for the differences and the feelings the eyes display. The feelings may also be related to facial expressions and the ways eyes show emotion. A story may be created to go with each pair of eyes. The object of the activity is to elicit the greatest possible amount of verbal expression, either for language remediation or articulation carryover.

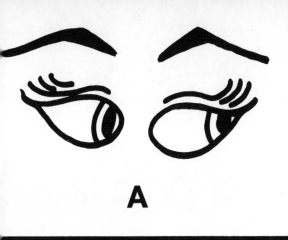

A

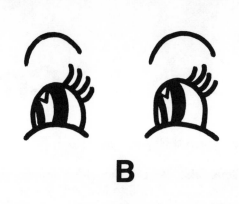

B

C

D

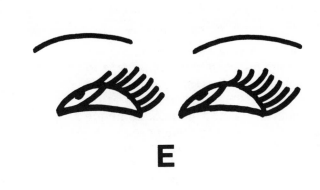

E

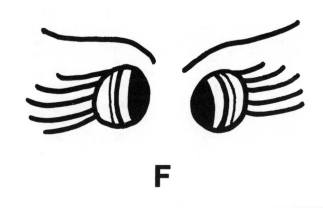

F

G

40 **What Do the Eyes See?**

41
Croquet

Suggested Grade Level: 1-6

Materials: Game sheet and marker for each player.
Plus and Minus Spinner.

Objectives: 1. The student will correctly articulate a target sound.

2. The student will complete sentences, use appropriate grammatical elements, or improve auditory sequential memory.

Method of Play

For Objective 1: Write stimulus words containing the target sound beneath each wicket. Distribute the game sheets and markers. Tell the players that they must spin the Plus and Minus Spinner to find out how many wickets they can pass through.

Example: Write *spin, sport, span,* and *speak* under the first four wickets. The first player spins and the spinner arrow stops at +3. The player moves ahead three wickets, saying *spin, sport, span.* The second player spins and the spinner arrow stops at +2. The player moves ahead two wickets, saying *spin, sport.* The first player spins again, gets -2, and retreats two spaces, saying *sport, spin.*

This game provides a great deal of repetition. To enter the game, players must spin so the spinner arrow stops on a number with a plus symbol. The first player to reach *finish* is the winner.

For Objective 2: Distribute the game sheets and markers. Tell the players that they are to respond to your oral cues, spin their spinners, and pass through the wickets. The speed of progression through the wickets is based on the Plus and Minus Spinner. If working on sentence completion, the player must complete a stimulus sentence in order to take a turn. The task might require the player to supply the number of words corresponding to the number the spinner arrow stops at. For grammatic closure, give oral stimuli according to individual need. A player moves if the response is correct. When working with auditory sequential memory, either digits, words, or sentences may be the stimuli. Questions may also be used.

Example: What is the fourth word in this group?
Chair, table, candy, book, bell

41 Croquet

Start

Finish

42
Astronaut Game

Suggested Grade Level: 1-6

Materials: Game sheet and marker for each player.
1-4 Spinner.

Objectives: 1. The student will correctly articulate a target sound.

2. The student will form sentences.

Method of Play

For Objective 1: Write stimulus words containing the target sound on the spaces leading to the moon. Distribute the game sheets and markers. Starting at the bottom of the game sheet, players take turns spinning the 1-4 Spinner and moving along the path the specified number of spaces. Upon landing on a space, a player is required to correctly articulate the word on that space or to use the word in a sentence and produce the target sound correctly. The player might be asked to say the word the number of times indicated by the spinner arrow. If correct, the marker remains on that space. If the response is incorrect, the marker is moved back one space and the student responds to the stimulus word on that space. The game continues until a player reaches the moon and wins the game.

For Objective 2: Select stimuli to elicit correct grammatical structures, specific syntactical elements, descriptive words or emotional language. Write stimulus words on the game sheet. Distribute the sheets and markers. The game is played as described for Objective 1 except that the player is required to form sentences using the stimulus words. These sentences may be simple, compound, or complex, declarative or interrogative. The first player to reach the moon wins the game.

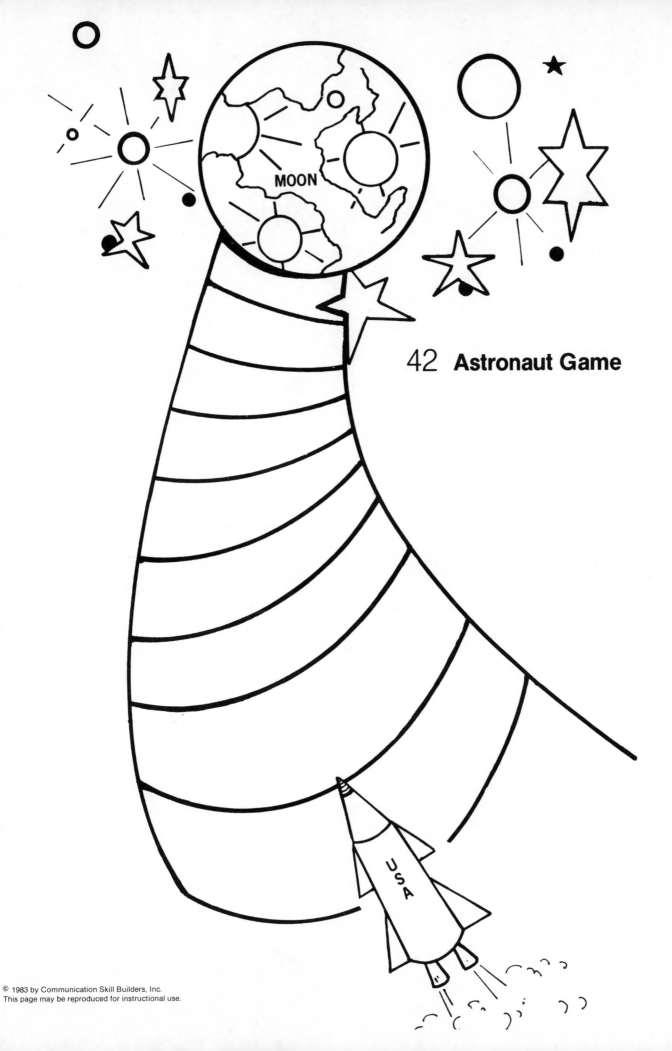

42 Astronaut Game

All the Games Kids Like
1-8

43
Pop My Balloon

Suggested Grade Level: 1-8

Materials: Game sheet and pencil for each player.
1-6 Spinner.

Objectives: 1. The student will correctly articulate a target sound.
  2. The student will use antonyms, synonyms, homonyms, adjectives, adverbs, etc.
  3. The student will use classification.

Method of Play

For Objective 1: Write a stimulus word containing the target sound on each balloon. Distribute the game sheets and pencils. A player selects a balloon and spins the 1-6 Spinner. The number the spinner arrow stops on is the number of times the stimulus word on the selected balloon must be articulated correctly.

Example: The first player selects balloon 12. The stimulus word is *stand,* and the spinner arrow stops on 6. The player must then say *stand* six times correctly. If successful, the player records a six in balloon 12. If the player produces only four correct responses, a 4 is recorded on that space.

Play ends when all the balloons have been marked. Points are totaled to determine the winner.

For Objective 2: A spinner is not required for this version of the game. Write a stimulus word on each balloon. Distribute the game sheets and pencils. Instruct the players to listen carefully as you call out the number of a balloon. All the players look for the selected balloon. The first to locate it calls out the answer to the stimulus on that space. If the response is correct, the player marks that balloon. The first player to mark all the balloons is the winner.

For Objective 3: Write a category on each balloon. Distribute the game sheets and pencils. Each player in turn spins the 1-6 Spinner and, starting with balloon 1, provides as many items in that category as the spinner indicates.

Example: The spinner arrow stops on 3 and the category in balloon 1 is *animals.* The player names three animals. If all three are correct, a 3 is recorded in balloon 1 on that player's game sheet. The next player spins a 6 and names six animals. If correct, a 6 is recorded on balloon 1 on that player's game sheet. When all the balloons have been marked, total each player's points to determine the winner.

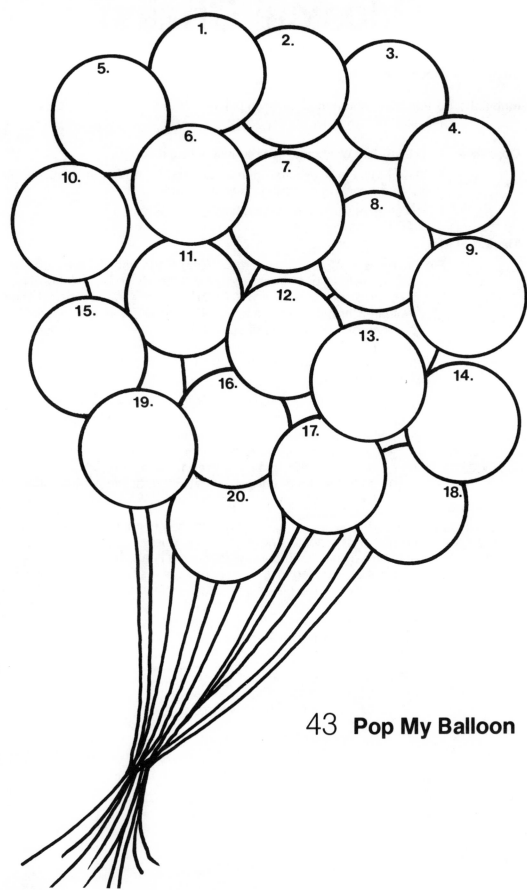

43 **Pop My Balloon**

44
Musical Chairs

Suggested Grade Level: 1-8

Materials: Game sheet and pencil for each player.
1-6 Spinner.

Objectives: 1. The student will correctly articulate a target sound.

             2. The student will use antonyms, synonyms, homonyms, adjectives, adverbs, rhyming words, classification, etc.

             3. The student will use a stimulus word in a sentence.

Method of Play

For Objective 1: Write words containing the target sound on each chair. Distribute the game sheets and pencils. Establish a time limit. Players take turns spinning the 1-6 Spinner, selecting the number of chairs indicated, and responding to the stimulus on each chair. Record the number of correct responses on the player's game sheet. If a response is incorrect, write that word on the game sheet for further practice. When the time is up, total the number of correct responses. The player with the highest total is the winner.

For Objective 2: Write the stimulus words on the chairs. Distribute the game sheets and pencils. The first player selects a chair and responds to the stimulus. If correct, the player spins the 1-6 Spinner to determine the number of points that turn was worth. These points are recorded below the chair. Play continues until all players have marked all the chairs on their sheets or until the allotted time has passed. Points are totaled to determine the winner.

For Objective 3: Write stimulus words on the chairs. Distribute the game sheets and pencils. The first player selects a chair and forms a sentence using the stimulus word on that chair. The sentence may be declarative, interrogative, or may include a specified question word or verb tense. If the player provides an acceptable response, the 1-6 Spinner is used to determine the number of points earned. These are recorded on that chair. Points are totaled when all the chairs have been used. The player with the highest total is the winner.

All the Games Kids Like
2-6

45
Camping Trip

Suggested Grade Level: 2-6

Materials: Game sheet and marker for each player.
1-4 Spinner.

Objectives: 1. The student will correctly articulate a target sound.

2. The student will use classification.

3. The student will use verbal expression.

Method of Play

For Objective 1: Write stimuli containing the target sound on the spaces. Stimuli may be single words, phrases, sentences, slogans, or ad copy suitable for billboard display. They may or may not follow the camping theme. Distribute the game sheets and markers. Place the markers on *start*. Players take turns spinning the 1-4 Spinner and moving the indicated number of spaces. The player must correctly articulate all words passed.

  Example: The spinner arrow stops on 3. The player moves three spaces, saying the stimulus on each space passed, stopping on the third space.

A player could be required to use stimulus words in a sentence pertinent to camping. Players proceed around the game sheet as time allows. Just before time is up, let each player have one or two more turns. The first player to reach *finish* is the winner.

For Objective 2: Write a category on each billboard. Distribute the game sheets and markers. Place the markers on *start*. Each player in turn spins the 1-4 Spinner, moves the indicated number of spaces, and names an object that fits the category the marker lands on. Play continues around the game sheet as time allows. Just before time is up, give each player one or two more turns. The first one to reach *finish* wins the game.

For Objective 3: Write a stimulus word on each billboard. Distribute the game sheets and markers. Establish a time limit. The method of play is as described for Objective 2 except that players are to describe the stimulus word on each billboard, providing as many aspects as possible. A point is given for each valid descriptive item. Record the points on the game sheets. When the allotted time has elapsed, points are totaled. The player with the most points is the winner.

45 Camping Trip

Finish

Start

46
Silly Snake

Suggested Grade Level: 2-6

Materials: Game sheet and marker for each player.
1-4 Spinner.

Objectives: 1. The student will correctly articulate a target sound.

2. The student will use antonyms, synonyms, homonyms, question words, rhyming words, etc.

Method of Play

For Objective 1: Write stimulus words containing the target sound on the spaces on the snake. Distribute the game sheets and markers. Place the markers on *start.* Players take turns spinning the 1-4 Spinner and moving the indicated number of spaces. When a marker lands on a space, the stimulus word on that space must be correctly articulated as many times as the spinner indicated. The player records the number of correct productions in that space.

Example: The spinner arrow stops on 3. The player moves three spaces. The stimulus word on the third space is *shape.* The player articulates it correctly three times and writes the the number 3 on that space. If the player produces only two correct responses, the number 2 is written on the space.

When all the players have reached *finish,* total the points to determine the winner.

For Objective 2: Write stimulus words on the snake. Distribute the game sheets and markers. Players in turn spin the 1-4 Spinner, move the indicated number of spaces, and respond to the stimulus word in the last space. If correct, the player records 1 point on that space. When all players have reached *finish,* points are totaled to determine the winner.

46 Silly Snake

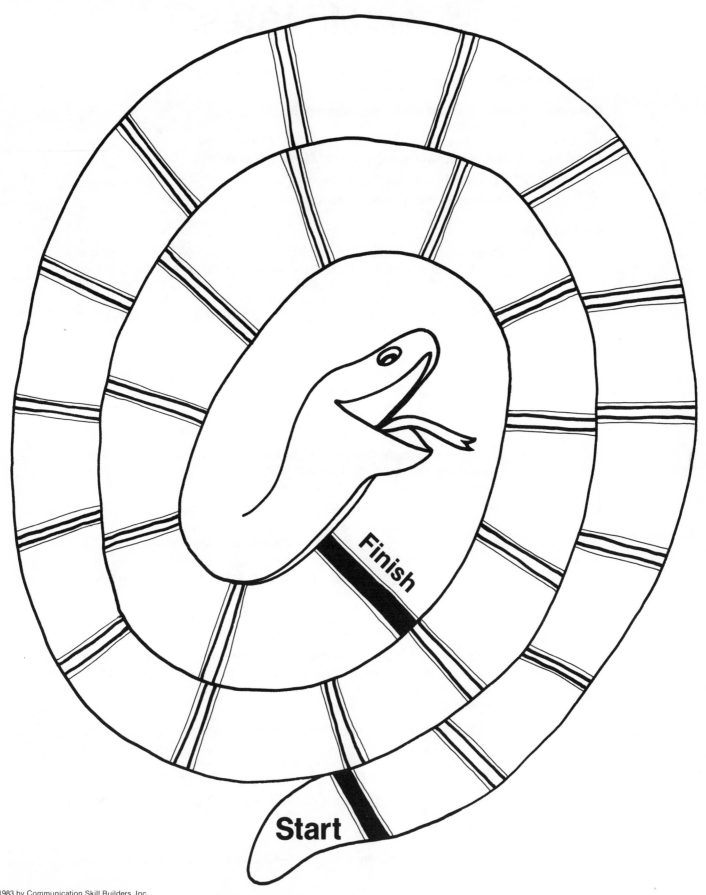

Finish

Start

47
Musical Notes

Suggested Grade Level: 2-6

Materials: Game sheet and pencil for each player.
1-6 Spinner.

Objectives: 1. The student will correctly articulate a target sound.

2. The student will use classification.

3. The student will use descriptive words.

Method of Play

For Objective 1: Write stimulus words containing the target sound below each space (musical bar). Distribute the game sheets and pencils. Players take turns selecting a space, spinning the 1-6 Spinner, and articulating the stimulus word the number of times indicated by the spinner. Record a point for each correct production by drawing a musical note on that space.

Example: If the spinner arrow stops at 5, the player says the stimulus word five times. If all five productions are correct, the player draws five musical notes in that space.

The game ends when all spaces on the game sheet have been used. The player with the most musical notes is the winner.

For Objective 2: Write a category below each space (musical bar). Distribute the game sheets and pencils. Each player in turn selects a space and spins the 1-6 Spinner. The player then provides the number of items in the category according to the number indicated on the spinner.

Example: The first player chooses *clothing.* The spinner arrow stops at 6. The player must name six articles of clothing. Only four responses are correct so the player draws four musical notes on that space.

When all spaces have been used, the game ends. The winner is the player with the most musical notes.

For Objective 3: Write a noun below each space (musical bar). Distribute the game sheets and pencils. The game is played as described for Objective 1 except that the player provides descriptive words for the stimuli.

Example: A player selects *table.* The spinner arrow stops at 3. The player then says, "A table is wood, heavy, and pretty." The player draws one note on that space for each correct response. In this case, the player draws three notes.

The game ends when all spaces have been used. Notes are totaled to determine the winner.

Variation:
For an easier game, use the 1-4 Spinner, which requires fewer responses.

47 Musical Notes

48
Speech Train

Suggested Grade Level: 2-6

Materials: Game sheet and marker for each player.
1-4 Spinner.

Objectives: 1. The student will correctly articulate a target sound.

   2. The student will use synonyms, antonyms, adjectives, etc.

Method of Play

For Objective 1: Write stimulus words containing the target sound on the railroad-track spaces. Distribute the game sheets and markers. Players take turns spinning the 1-4 Spinner, moving the indicated number of spaces, and saying each stimulus word passed. If the target sounds are produced correctly, the player moves across all spaces indicated. If an error is made, the marker stays on that space.

Example: The spinner arrow stops at 3. The player moves three spaces saying, *sink, sap, sit.* The second player spins and the spinner arrow stops on 4. The player moves four spaces saying, *sink, sap, sit, set.* If the second player makes an error on *sap,* the marker stays on the second space and the player waits there for the next turn. If a player lands on a space occupied by another player, the first player can be "bumped" back to the engine.

The game ends when a player reaches the *station* and is declared the winner.

For Objective 2: Write the desired stimuli on the railroad-track spaces. Distribute the game sheets and markers. A player in turn spins the 1-4 Spinner, moves the indicated number of spaces, and responds to the stimulus word in the space the marker lands on. The first player to reach the *station* is the winner.

116

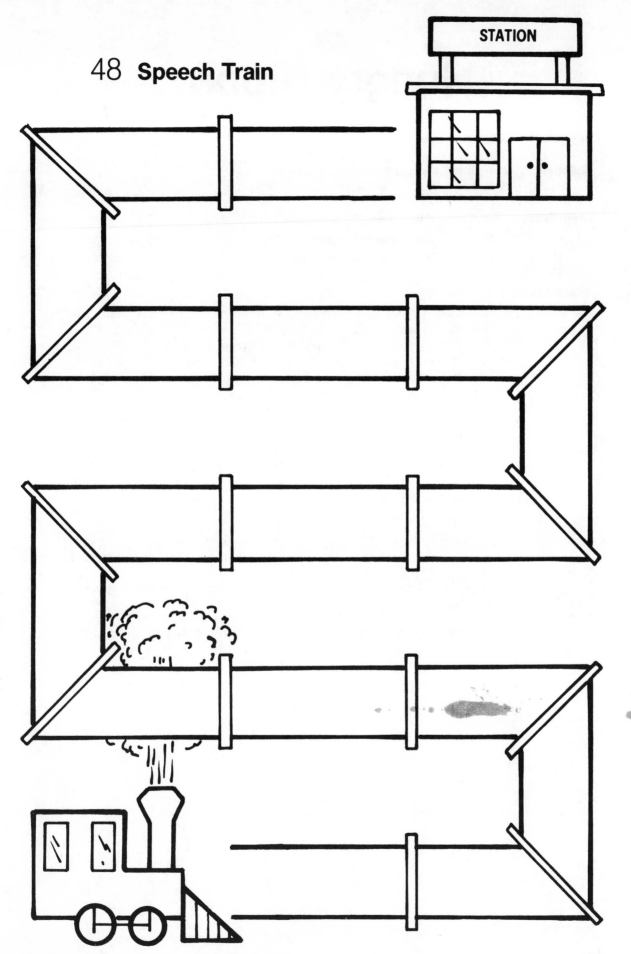

48 **Speech Train**

STATION

49
Hungry Hippo

Suggested Grade Level: 2-6

Materials: Game sheet and pencil for each player.
1-4 Spinner.

Objectives: 1. The student will correctly articulate a target sound.

2. The student will use antonyms, synonyms, adjectives, adverbs, etc.

3. The student will use classification.

Method of Play

For Objective 1: Write stimulus words on the rocks and leaves. Distribute the game sheets and pencils. Players take turns selecting a rock or a leaf and spinning the 1-4 Spinner. The player correctly articulates the selected word the number of times indicated by the spinner. If the responses are correct, the player marks that space off. The game ends when each player has marked the entire sheet.

For Objective 2: Write stimulus words on each rock and leaf. Distribute the game sheets and pencils. In turn, players select a rock or leaf and respond to the stimulus. If the response is correct, the player spins the 1-4 Spinner. The number indicated is the number of points the player receives for that turn. Record the points on the space with the stimulus word. When all players have completed their sheets, total the points to determine the winner.

For Objective 3: Write a category on each rock or leaf. Distribute the game sheets and pencils. A player selects a category and spins the 1-4 Spinner. The number indicated is the number of responses the player must give in that category. A point is recorded for each correct response.

Example: The category selected is *colors.* The spinner arrow stops at 3 so the player must name three colors. If correct, the player writes a 3 in that space.

When all the spaces have been used, the points are totaled. The player with the most points is the winner.

49 **Hungry Hippo**

50
Recess

Suggested Grade Level: 2-6

Materials: Game sheet and marker for each player.
1-4 Spinner.

Objectives: 1. The student will correctly articulate a target sound.

               2. The student will use classification.

               3. The student will use synonyms, antonyms, homonyms, etc.

Method of Play

For Objective 1: Write a stimulus word on each blank space. Distribute the game sheets and markers. Place the markers on *go.* Players take turns spinning the 1-4 Spinner and moving the indicated number of spaces. A player is required to respond to each stimulus word passed, stopping on that space if a response is incorrect. Recess is over and the game ends when a player completes the path and arrives at *go* again. The spinner arrow must stop at the exact number of spaces needed to reach *go.* If a player needs to make three jumps to reach *go,* the spinner arrow must stop on 1, 2, or 3 for the player to move. If the spinner arrow stops on 4, the player stays on the same space, repeats the stimulus word, and waits for another turn.

For Objective 2: Write categories on the blank spaces. Give each player a game sheet and a marker. The markers are placed on *go.* A player spins the 1-4 Spinner, moves the indicated number of spaces, and gives the indicated number of responses.

    Example: If the spinner arrow stops on 4, the player moves the marker four spaces, and gives four responses to the stimulus word on the final space.

A point may be awarded for each correct response. The first player to go all around the path and arrive at *go* again is the winner.

For Objective 3: Write stimuli on the blank spaces. Distribute the game sheets and markers. Play the game as described for Objective 1. You may wish to have the players go around the path more than once. If so, tell the players that to win they must go around two (or three or four) times and return each time to *go.*

Go

Throw sand. Miss a turn.

Swing high. Go ahead 1 space.

Catch a ball. Go ahead 2 spaces.

Push a friend down. Go back 2 spaces.

Climb monkey bars. Go ahead 2 spaces.

Get to class on time. Go ahead 1 space.

Your team wins a game. Take an extra turn.

51
Fox in the Forest

Suggested Grade Level: 2-6

Materials: Game sheet and 11 markers for each player.
Plus and Minus Spinner.

Objectives: 1. The student will correctly articulate a target sound.

2. The student will use classification.

Method of Play

For Objective 1: Write a stimulus word on each tree. Give each player a
game sheet and 11 markers. Players place one of their markers on
start. A player must spin a number with a plus symbol on the Plus and
Minus Spinner in order to start. Players take turns spinning the
spinner and moving the indicated number of spaces in one direction
or the other. Each word must be produced correctly as it is passed. If
a response is incorrect, the player pays a marker to the fox. The first
player to reach *Grandma's house* without losing any markers is the
winner and wins all the markers from the fox. If a player loses all 11
markers, more markers may be borrowed from the bank and the
player plays with a negative score.

For Objective 2: Write a category on each tree. Distribute the game sheets
and give 11 markers to each player. The game is played as described
for Objective 1, but the player does not have to respond to each
stimulus word passed. The player responds only to the one the
marker lands on. The fox receives a token for each incorrect
response. The first player to reach *Grandma's house* with all 11
tokens is the winner.

Grandma's House

Start

52
Wagon Wheel

Suggested Grade Level: 2-6

Materials: Game sheet and pencil for each player.
1-4 Spinner.

Objective: The student will use descriptive words.

Method of Play

Give each player a game sheet and a pencil. Each player in turn selects a word from the wheel. The player must use that word to describe something or someone, preferably in a complete sentence.

Example: A player selects *funny* and says, "I saw a funny clown."

If the response is appropriate, the player spins the spinner to determine the number of points won for that turn. Record points in the stimulus space on the wheel. The game ends when all the spaces have been used. The player with the most points is the winner.

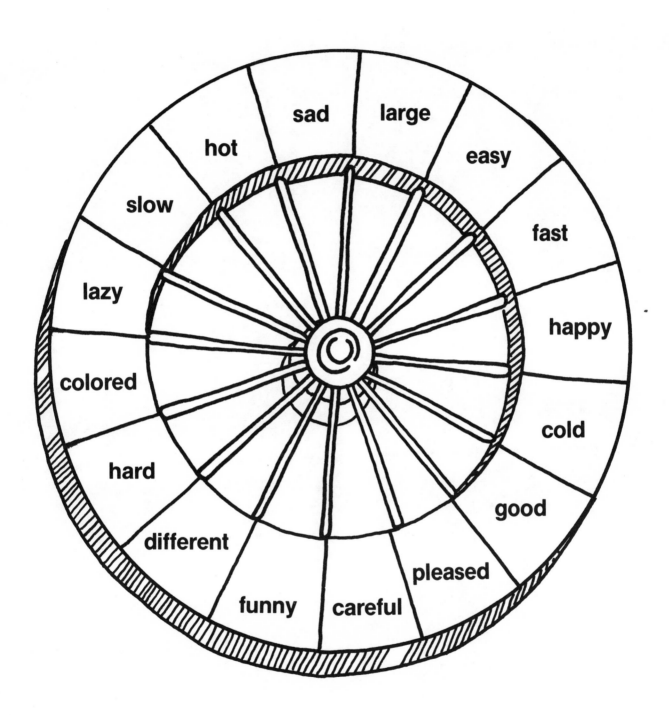

All the Games Kids Like
3-6

53
Spin-a-Sound

Suggested Grade Level: 3-6

Materials: Game sheet and pencil for each player.
Spin-a-Sound Spinner.

Objectives: 1. The student will correctly articulate a target sound.

2. The student will form a sentence.

Method of Play

For Objective 1: Write stimulus words on the spaces. Distribute the game sheets and pencils. Players take turns spinning the spinner and making the indicated moves. A player articulates the stimulus word in the designated space and, if correct, marks that space on the game sheet. The object of the game is to mark off all the spaces on the sheet.

Example: The spinner arrow stops on *Go to 3.* After correctly saying the stimulus word on space 3, the player marks it off on the sheet.

If a response is incorrect, the player does not mark off that space. The first player to mark all the spaces is the winner. If a player spins a number already marked off, the word in that space might be repeated, placed in a sentence, or articulated three times.

For Objective 2: Write a noun, verb, adverb, or other part of speech on each space. Distribute the game sheets and pencils. A player spins the spinner and follows the directions indicated. The player provides a sentence for the stimulus word. If correct, the space is marked off. When a player lands on a space that has already been marked off, the required response may be to elicit another sentence or a description of the stimulus word. The first player to mark off all the circles is the winner.

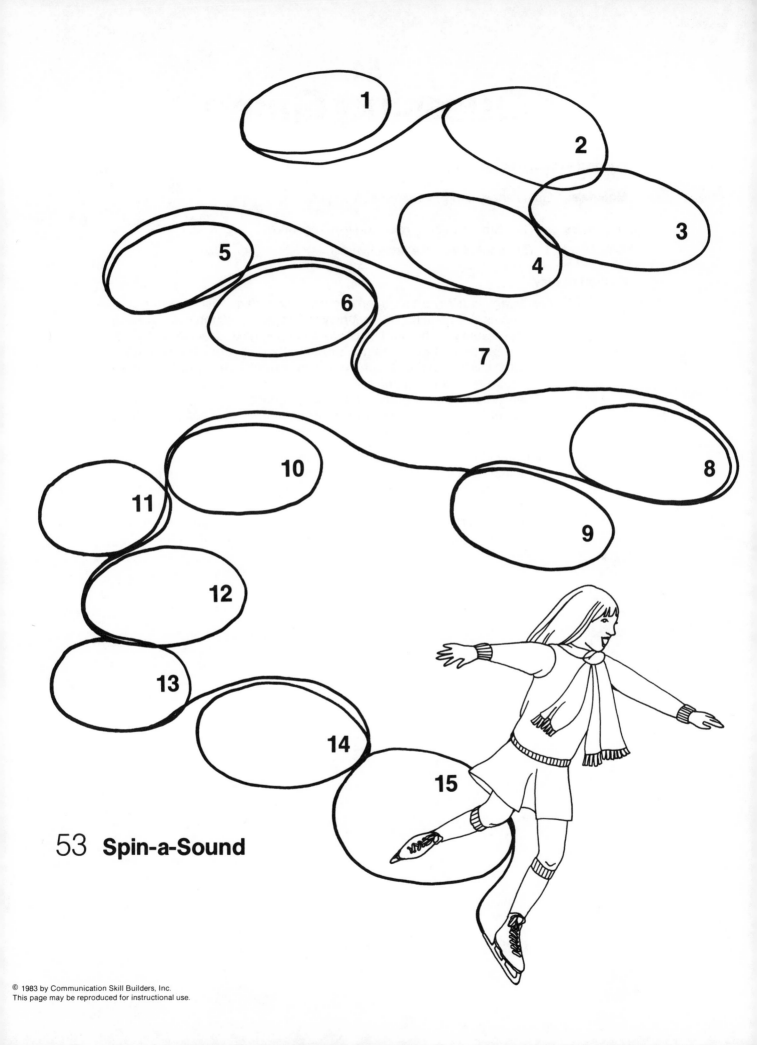

53 **Spin-a-Sound**

54
Guessing Game

Suggested Grade Level: 3-6

Materials: Game sheet and pencil for each player.

Objectives: 1. The student will improve auditory reception.
                  2. The student will use adjectives.

Method of Play

For Objective 1: Write a noun on each question mark. Distribute the game sheets and pencils. The first player selects a question mark but does not reveal which one. The player then begins to describe the object named on that question mark to the other players who try to guess what it is. When the object is guessed correctly, that question mark is crossed off on all game sheets. Both the player who gave the clues and the one who guessed correctly record a point on their game sheets. Play stops when all the question marks have been crossed off. The player with the most points is the winner.

For Objective 2: Write a noun on each question mark. Distribute the game sheets and pencils. Players take turns selecting a question mark and providing as many adjectives as possible to describe the object named there. If six correct responses are given, the number 6 is written on that question mark. After each player has responded to each question mark, the points are totaled to determine the winner.

54 **Guessing Game**

55
Lucky 7

Suggested Grade Level: 3-6

Materials: Game sheet and marker for each player.
1-4 Spinner.

Objectives: 1. The student will correctly articulate a target sound.
2. The student will use antonyms, synonyms, homonyms, adjectives, adverbs, etc.

Method of Play

For Objective 1: Write words containing the target sound on the blank spaces *and* on the spaces containing a 7. Distribute the game sheets and markers. The first player spins the 1-4 Spinner and moves the marker the indicated number of spaces. The player articulates the word in the space the marker landed on. If the response is correct, the player receives a point. If incorrect, the marker is moved back one space and the player articulates the word in that space. If a player lands on a 7, the word in that space is articulated seven times. If all seven productions are correct, the player receives seven points as a bonus. When all the players have completed their game sheets, total the points. The player with the most points is the winner.

For Objective 2: Write stimulus words on the blank spaces *and* on the 7 spaces. Give each player a game sheet and a marker. The first player spins the 1-4 Spinner, moves the indicated number of spaces, and responds correctly to the stimulus word. A correct response wins a point. If an error is made, the player receives no point for that turn. A player landing on a 7 wins a bonus of seven points if the response to the stimulus in that space is correct. When all the players have completed their game sheets, total the points to determine the winner.

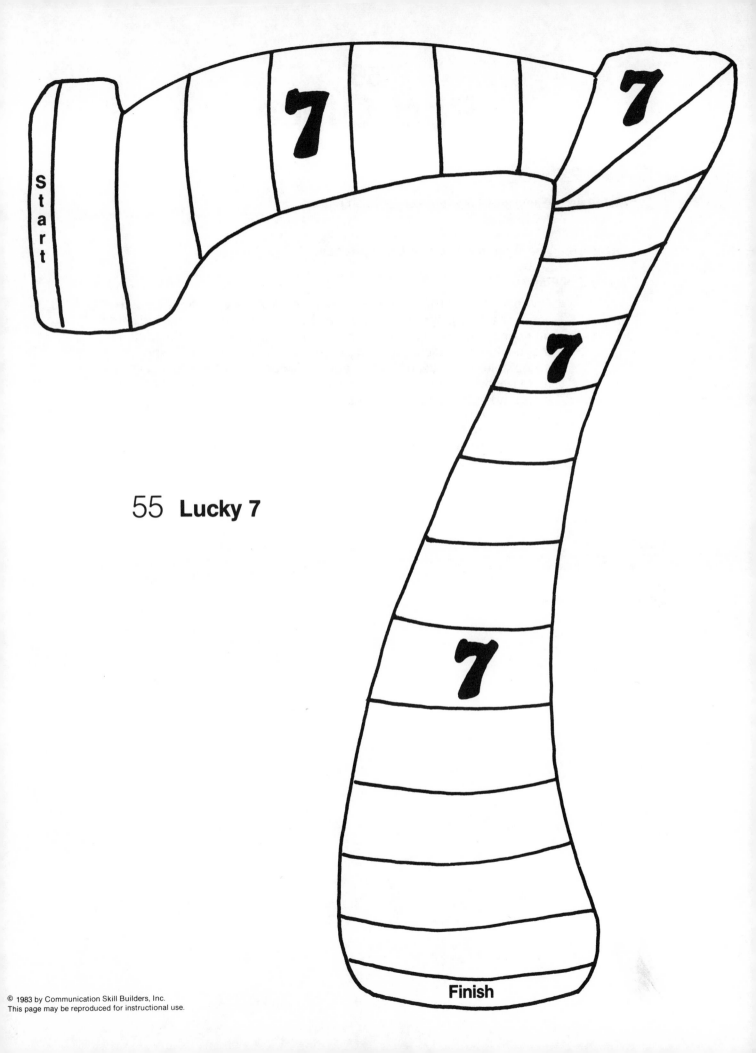

Start

7

7

7

7

55 **Lucky 7**

Finish

56
Post Office

Suggested Grade Level: 3-6

Materials: Game sheet and marker for each player.
1-6 Spinner.

Objective: The student will use verbal expression.

Method of Play

Give each player a game sheet and marker. Each marker is to be placed on *start*. The first player spins the 1-6 Spinner and moves the indicated number of spaces. The player then tells what could be written in a letter to the person or place mentioned on that space. If the response is acceptable, the player receives a point, although points are not necessary for this activity. Encourage the players to discuss and compare their ideas. If the marker lands on a space designating something other than a person, the player takes an extra turn but must first tell what the phrase on that space means. Play continues until all players have returned to start or until time is up. If points are given, total them to determine the winner.

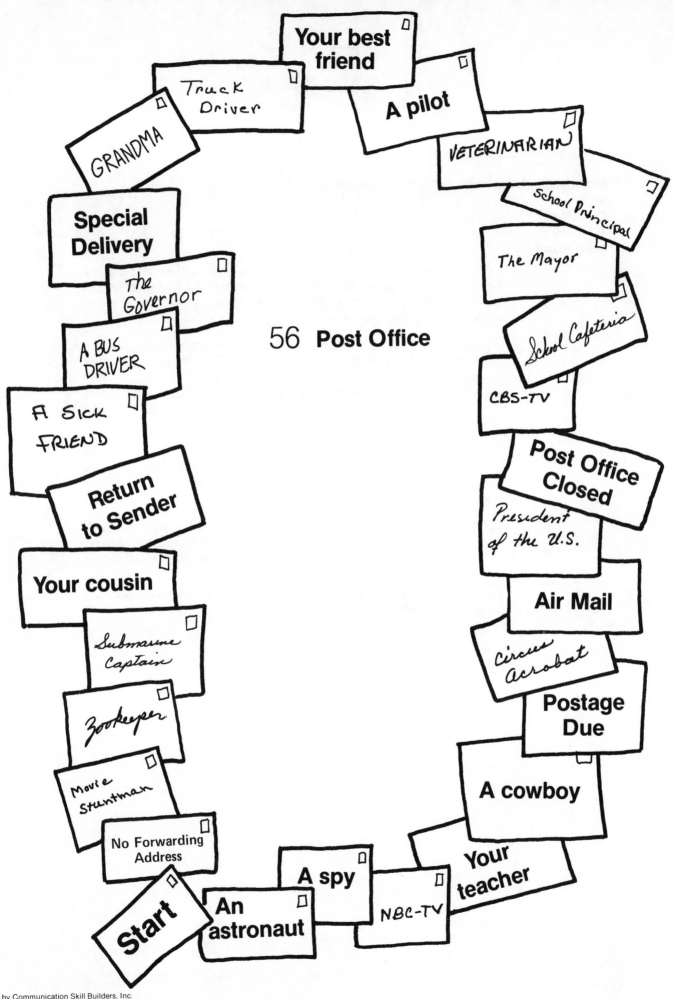

56 **Post Office**

57
Labels

Suggested Grade Level: 3-6

Materials: Game sheet and pencil for each player.

Objective: The student will classify objects.

Methods of Play

A. In the first method of play, give each player a game sheet and pencil. Select a label from the game sheet. The players take turns naming as many objects as they can in the selected category. The label is then marked off on their game sheets.

B. A second method of play is to ask a player to select a label and name as many objects as possible in that category. The number of correct responses is then recorded on that label. One point is given for each correct response. It is then the next player's turn. When all the labels have been marked, players total their points. The one with the most points is the winner.

C. A third method of play is to have each player in turn select a label without revealing the choice to the group. The player then names as many objects in that category as possible until another player guesses the label or category.

Example: A player selects a label and says, "Lettuce, tomatoes, peanut butter, jelly." Another player interrupts and says, "Things you put in a sandwich!" Both players receive a point.

Labels may be selected more than once. When time is up, points are totaled to determine the winner.

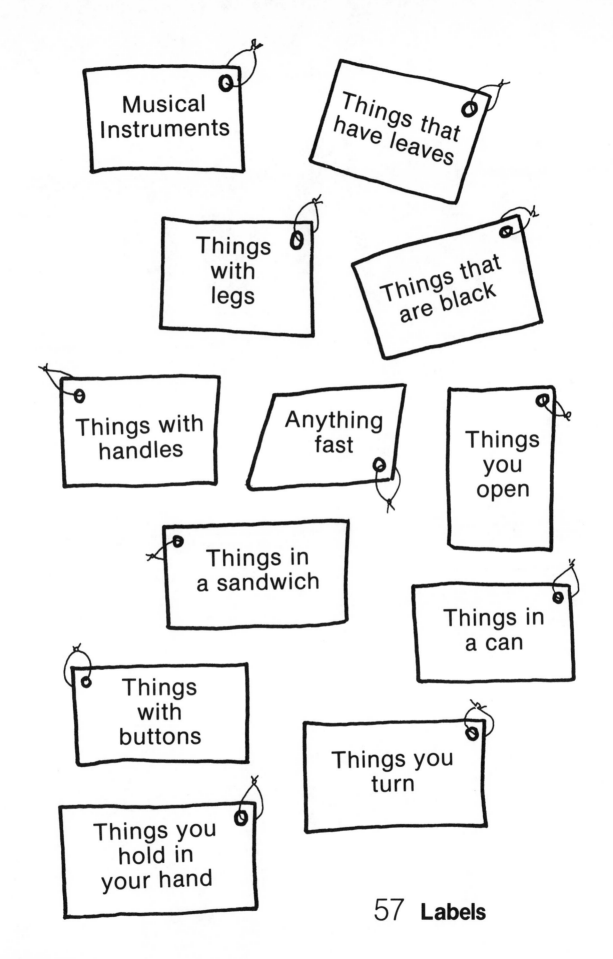

Musical Instruments

Things that have leaves

Things with legs

Things that are black

Things with handles

Anything fast

Things you open

Things in a sandwich

Things in a can

Things with buttons

Things you turn

Things you hold in your hand

57 **Labels**

All the Games Kids Like
3-8

58
Prime Time

Suggested Grade Level: 3-8

Materials: Game sheet and pencil for each player.
Paper Emmy awards.

Objectives: 1. The student will correctly articulate a target sound in spontaneous speech.
2. The student will use verbal expression.
3. The student will improve auditory sequential memory.

Method of Play

For Objective 1: Give the players game sheets and pencils. Ask them to draw a picture representing their favorite television show on the TV screen and include items from that show that contain the target sound. When the drawings are complete, each player names the target-sound words and tells about the show. The player may describe an episode, a character, or the show's theme. The object is to use the target sound correctly. Write the incorrect productions on the game sheet for later practice. Award a paper Emmy to the players who complete the activity without an error.

For Objective 2: Distribute the game sheets and pencils. Each player draws a picture that illustrates a favorite television show. The player then tells something about the show by describing the illustration. The story can be told, the theme discussed, or the characters described. Other players may offer opinions about the show.

Variation:
Players could also create their own television series, illustrate it on the game sheet, and describe it to the group. After the descriptions, the players vote on the best show and a paper Emmy is awarded to the winner.

For Objective 3: Distribute the game sheets and pencils. Tell the players to listen carefully to your directions, which may be in combinations of two, three, or four, in sentences or in riddles.

Examples: 1. "Draw a table at the bottom of the TV screen, then put some flowers in a vase on the table." When this has been done, give the next set of directions: "Draw a cat with a happy face under the table and have his paws holding a ball of yarn."
2. "Draw a cat, a penny, a fork, and a hat."

Check all the game sheets and give a paper Emmy to the players who have correctly followed all your directions.

59
Book Covers

Suggested Grade Level: 3-8

Materials: Game sheet and pencil for each player.

Objectives: 1. The student will correctly articulate a target sound.

             2. The student will use verbal expression.

             3. The student will improve auditory sequential memory.

Method of Play

For Objective 1: Distribute the game sheets and pencils. Ask each player in turn to provide a book title containing the target sound. If the response is correct, the player writes the title on a book cover. If a response is incorrect, the player waits for the next turn and tries again. The first player to mark all the book covers is the winner. Further practice may be given by having the players talk about the contents of the books.

Variation:

Players may prefer to illustrate the book covers and not write the titles.

For Objective 2: Give each player a game sheet and pencil. Ask each player to make up a book idea and tell something about it. Each player tells the title, author, and something about the plot or characters. Then the player draws the cover illustration on a book cover on the game sheet. The object is to complete the game sheet.

Variation:

Write a stimulus word on each book cover before distributing the game sheets. A player in turn uses the stimulus word in a book title, tells what the story might be about, something of the main character, and any other desired aspect. If the response is appropriate, the player marks the book cover on the game sheet. The object is to mark all the book covers.

For Objective 3: Dictate a series of three or four words. The players write the words on the book covers in the order given.

Example: Ask the players to listen carefully and write what you dictate. Give the stimulus words, "Book, apple, candy, dog." Each player records these words on one book cover.

If correct, players mark their book covers. The object is to mark all the book covers on the sheet. When the book covers are all marked, ask each player to select one and compose a title using all the words on that cover.

Example: The Dog Who Loves to Eat Books, Candy, and Apples

59 Book Covers

60
Billboard

Suggested Grade Level: 3-8

Materials: Game sheet and crayons for each player.

Objectives: 1. The student will correctly articulate a target sound.

2. The student will use verbal expression.

Method of Play

For Objective 1: Distribute the game sheets and crayons. Tell the players to pretend they are in the advertising business and they have a product to sell. Each product must contain the target sound. The players are to rent a billboard and draw an imaginative and eye-catching ad for their product. Establish a time limit. When the billboards have been completed or when the time is up, each player presents a sales pitch, being very careful to use the target sound correctly during the entire presentation. Record the errors on the game sheets for further practice.

For Objective 2: Begin the game as described for Objective 1. After the drawings are complete, each player describes the billboard, tells where it would be located, and then presents a sales pitch for the product. This is more fun when the products are imaginary or contrived such as "Calluses for Ordinary Feet" or "Superific Space Soap and Washcloth Combination." Encourage the other players to ask questions after each presentation.

60 Billboard

61
Basketball

Suggested Grade Level: 3-8

Materials: Game sheet and pencil for each player.

Objectives: 1. The student will correctly articulate a target sound.

2. The student will use adjectives, adverbs, selected verb tense, classification, antonyms, etc.

Method of Play

For Objective 1: Write a stimulus word on each basketball. Distribute the game sheets and pencils. Players take turns selecting a basketball, saying the stimulus word, and if correct, marking that basketball. The first player to mark all the basketballs is the winner. Words can be used in sentences or repeated a specified number of times.

Variation:

This game may also be played with two players as a tic-tac-toe game. The first player who marks three basketballs in a row in any direction is the winner.

For Objective 2: Play the game as described for Objective 1 except that the stimuli is delivered orally. If a response is correct, the player marks a basketball.

61 **Basketball**

62
Word Wheel

Suggested Grade Level: 3-8

Materials: Game sheet and pencil for each player.
1-6 Spinner.

Objectives: 1. The student will correctly articulate a target sound.

               2. The student will use adjectives, adverbs, synonyms, antonyms, etc.

Method of Play

For Objective 1: Write stimulus words containing the target sound on the spaces on the word wheel. Distribute the game sheets and pencils. Establish a time limit. Each player in turn spins the 1-6 Spinner twice and totals the two spins. A player spinning a 5 and then a 3 adds them together for a total of 8. The player responds to the stimulus on space 8 on the game sheet. If the response is correct, a point is recorded on that space. When the play period ends, points are totaled and the player with the most points wins.

For Objective 2: Write stimulus words in the spaces on the game sheet. Distribute the game sheets and pencils. Play the game as described for Objective 1, recording a point for each correct response. When a player responds incorrectly or cannot respond, the next player may attempt to answer, thus earning a point for being correct. Points are totaled at the end of the play period to determine the winner.

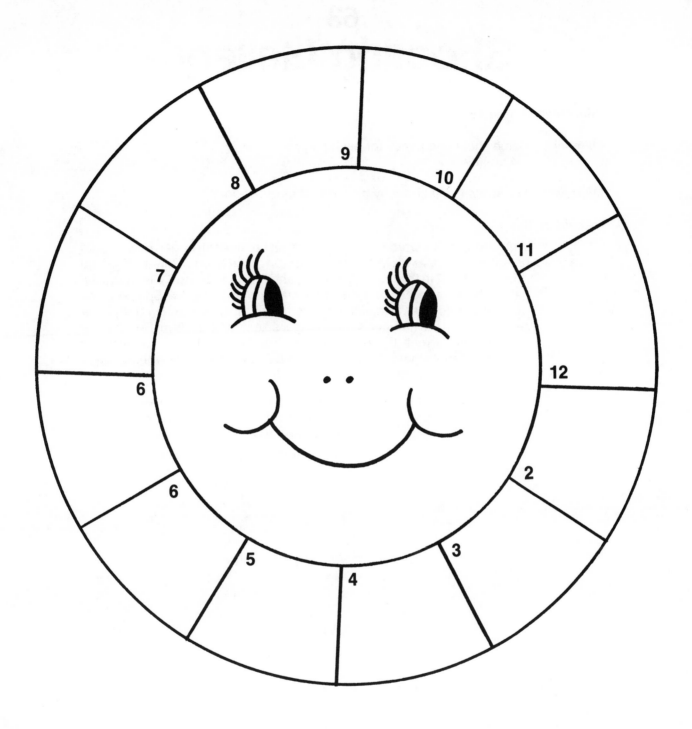

62 **Word Wheel**

63
Shooting Gallery

Suggested Grade Level: 3-8

Materials: Game sheet and pencil for each player.
1-4 Spinner.

Objective: The student will correctly articulate a target sound.

Method of Play

Write the stimulus words on the game sheet below each target. Row 4 could have the target sounds in the initial position of the words, Row 3 in the final position, Row 2 in the medial position, and Row 1 in blends. Distribute the game sheets and pencils. The first player spins the 1-4 Spinner. The number the spinner arrow stops at is the number of the row the player selects from. If the number is 2, the player selects a target from Row 2. If the response is correct, the player marks that target off and receives the number of points indicated under the target row. Play stops when a player has completed an entire row. Points are totaled to determine the winner.

Example: The spinner arrow stops at 3. The player selects a word from Row 3 and articulates it correctly. The player then marks that target off and receives three points.

The game can be played without the spinner by having the players select targets randomly.

Row 4

5 points

Row 3

3 points

Row 2

2 points

Row 1

1 point

63 **Shooting Gallery**

64
Memory Relay

Suggested Grade Level: 3-8

Materials: Game sheet and marker for each player.
1-6 Spinner.

Objectives: 1. The student will use classification.
2. The student will improve auditory sequential memory.

Method of Play

For Objective 1: Give each player a game sheet and a marker. Establish a time limit. Players take turns spinning the 1-6 Spinner, moving a marker the indicated number of spaces, and naming the number of category items indicated by the spin. A point is won for each correct item.

Example: The spinner arrow stops on 2. The player moves two spaces, landing on *something blue.* The player responds, "A dress, a chair, and a crayon" and receives three points on that space.

When the time is up, the player with the most points is the winner.

For Objective 2: Give each player a game sheet and a marker. The first player spins the 1-6 Spinner and moves the indicated number of spaces. The player names one item in the category the marker has landed on. The second player spins and moves the marker the indicated number of spaces. This player must then name the first player's item and add an item from the new category.

Example: The spinner arrow stops on 2. The first player moves two spaces to *something blue.* The player responds, "Shirt." The second player spins a 3, moves three spaces to *something with legs,* and says, "Shirt, dog." A third player spins a 1, moves one space to *anything hot,* and says, "Shirt, dog, iron."

Play continues until a player cannot recall a sequence. Some players prefer to continue playing, eliminating players as they forget items or the sequence of items. The last player to remain in the game is the winner.

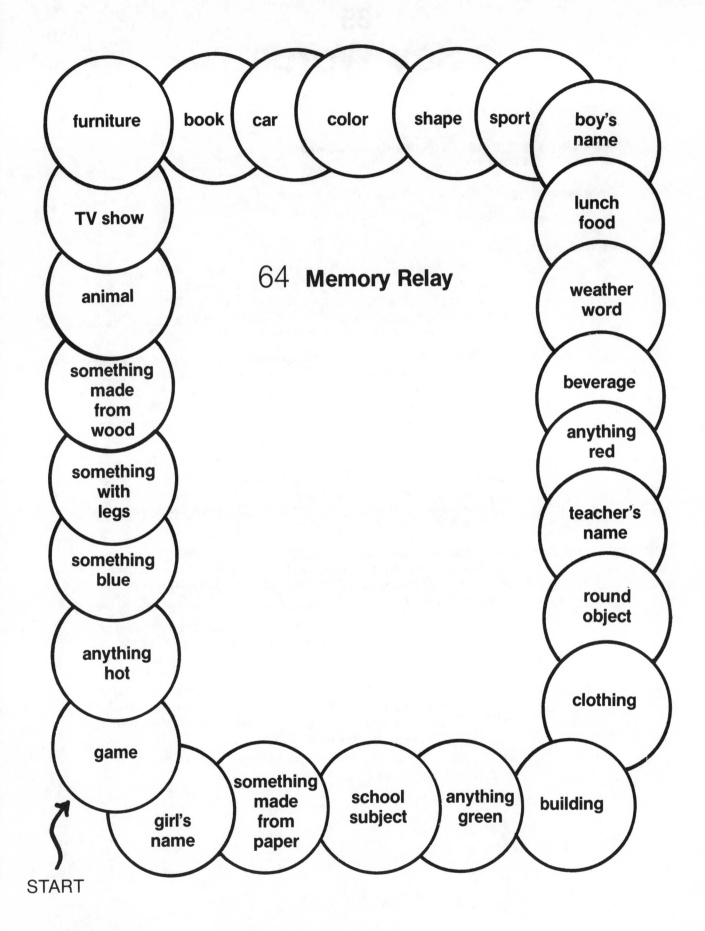

furniture   book   car   color   shape   sport   boy's name

lunch food

weather word

beverage

anything red

teacher's name

round object

clothing

building

64 **Memory Relay**

TV show

animal

something made from wood

something with legs

something blue

anything hot

game

girl's name

something made from paper

school subject

anything green

START

65
Say Words

Suggested Grade Level: 3-8

Materials: Game sheet and marker for each player.
1-4 Spinner.

Objectives: 1. The student will correctly articulate a target sound.

2. The student will use adjectives.

Method of Play

For Objective 1: Write a word containing the target sound on each space. Distribute the game sheets and markers. Players in turn spin the 1-4 Spinner, move the indicated number of spaces, and follow the directions on the space the marker lands on using the stimulus word. A point is given for each correct production.

> *Example:* The spinner arrow stops on 3. The player moves three spaces to *Say three words.* The stimulus word on that space is *ride.* The player says this three times correctly and records a 3 on that space for the number of correct responses. If the player had produced only two correct responses, two points would be recorded.

When landing on a space that says *Ask a question,* or *Say a sentence,* the player uses the stimulus word in a question or sentence respectively and is awarded five points. Play continues until all players have completed the game sheet. The player with the most points is the winner.

For Objective 2: The game is played as described in Objective 1, except that a noun is written on each space. Each player in turn provides descriptive words (adjectives) for each noun as directed on the space the marker lands on.

> *Example:* A player lands on a space that says *Say three words.* The stimulus word on that space is *car.* The player says, "Shiny, big, noisy" and records three points on that space—one point for each correct response. When required to *Ask a question* or *Say a sentence,* the player supplies an adjective for the noun and then uses both the adjective and noun in the question or sentence. If correct, the player receives five points.

When all players have completed their sheets, the points are totaled to determine the winner.

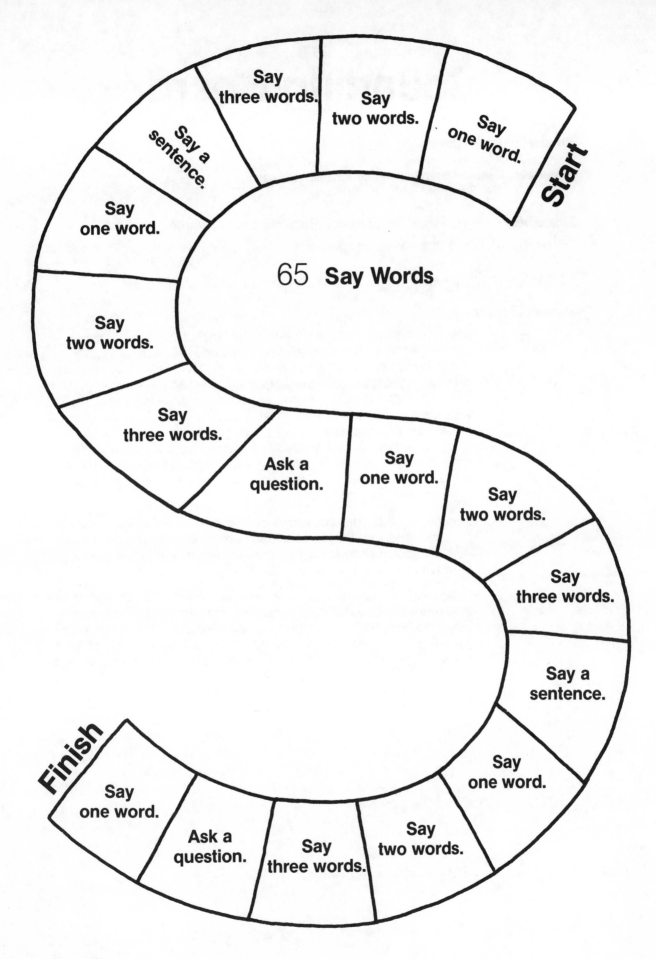

Say one word.

Say two words.

Say three words.

Say a sentence.

Say one word.

Say two words.

Say three words.

Ask a question.

Say one word.

Say two words.

Say three words.

Say a sentence.

Say one word.

Say two words.

Say three words.

Ask a question.

Say one word.

Start

Finish

65 **Say Words**

66
Sounding Board

Suggested Grade Level: 3-8

Materials: Game sheet and pencil for each player.
1-4 Spinner.

Objectives: 1. The student will correctly articulate a target sound.

2. The student will use adjectives, adverbs, antonyms, synonyms, verbs, etc.

3. The student will form questions and respond to questions.

Method of Play

For Objective 1: Write words containing the target sound on each space. Distribute the game sheets and pencils. Each player in turn spins the 1-4 Spinner twice to obtain two numbers. The player finds the first number at the top of the game sheet and the second number on the side. Then the stimulus word is located by following the paths of these two numbers until they meet in a space. The player articulates the word in that space. If correct, the player marks off that space. The first player to mark four spaces in a row horizontally, diagonally, or vertically is the winner. If a stimulus word is repeated, and the player has already marked it off, the word may be used in a sentence or another word may be given.

For Objective 2: Write stimulus words on the spaces. Distribute the game sheets and pencils. Play the game as described for Objective 1 except that instead of producing the stimulus word, the player gives an antonym, synonym, or other desired response.

For Objective 3: Write a stimulus word on each space. Play the game as described for Objective 1 except that the players form questions using the stimulus words. You may require that the questions begin with a specific question word or that the questions be written on the game sheet and answered by the other players. The first player to mark four spaces in a row is the winner.

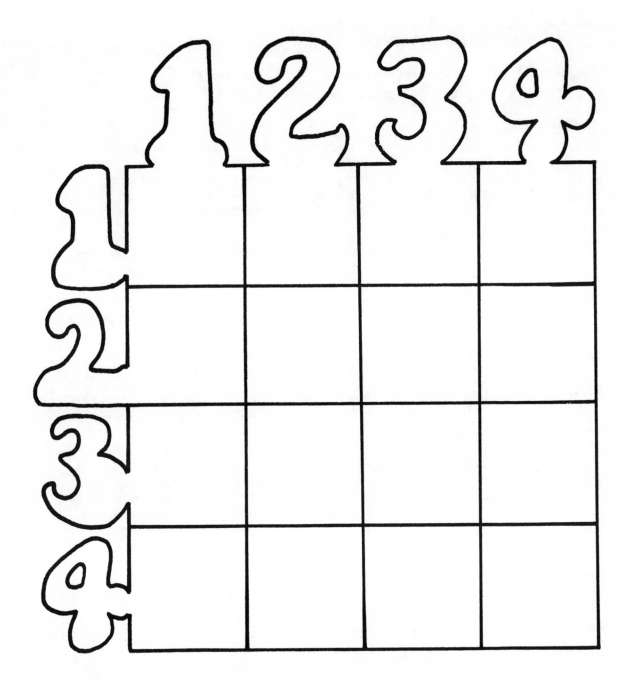

66 **Sounding Board**

67
Shopping Trip

Suggested Grade Level: 3-8

Materials: Game sheet and marker for each player.
Plus and Minus Spinner.

Objectives: 1. The student will correctly articulate a target sound.

2. The student will use classification.

Method of Play

For Objective 1: Stimulus words need not be written on the game sheet. Tell the players they are going to a department store or supermarket and will take turns naming an article they might buy in that store. The article must contain the target sound. Moves are determined by the Plus and Minus Spinner, which provides repetition of responses.

Example: The target sound is **S.** The players are shopping in a department store. The first player spins the spinner and the arrow stops at +3. Starting at *home,* the player moves three spaces and says, "Spy glass." The second player spins a +2, moves two spaces from *home,* and says, "Sweater." The first player spins a -2, moves back two spaces, and says, "Scarf."

A player must spin a number accompanied by a plus sign in order to start. The first player to reach the store is the winner.

Variation:
Players may be assigned different target sounds. If three players are in the game, one might be practicing **S,** another **CH,** and the third **K.**

For Objective 2: Tell the players they are going to a store such as a dress shop, a fruit store, a hardware store, a gift shop, a stationery store, etc. Distribute the game sheets and markers. The first player spins the Plus and Minus Spinner, moves the indicated number of spaces, and names something that can be purchased in that store. An added requirement might be to tell in which department the item can be bought. The first player to reach the store wins the game.

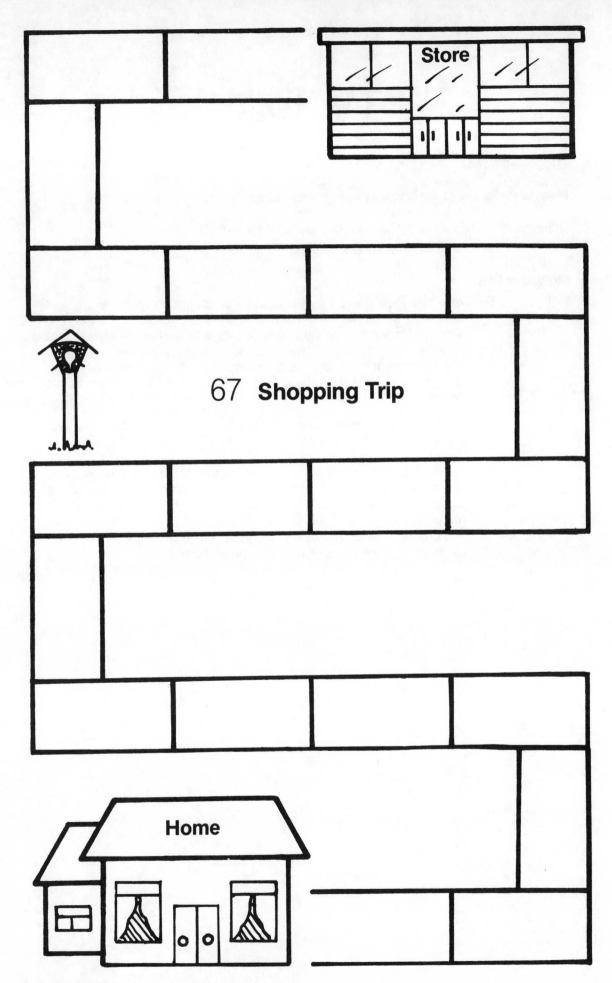

Store

67 **Shopping Trip**

Home

68
TV Talk

Suggested Grade Level: 3-8

Materials: Game sheet and crayons for each player.

Objectives: 1. The student will correctly articulate a target sound.
2. The student will use verbal expression.

Method of Play

For Objective 1: Give each player a game sheet and crayons. Players in turn name a television show containing the target sound. If the articulation is correct, the player draws or writes something related to that show on one of the TV screens. Older players might be required to write the title of the show and the name of a character from the show. Both the title and the character's name should contain the target sound.

For Objective 2: Distribute the game sheets and pencils or crayons. Ask each player to draw a picture depicting a TV show on each screen. When the drawings are complete, each player in turn describes one of the illustrations but does not reveal the name of the show. The other players guess the name of the show. A point is awarded to the player who guesses correctly. Points are totaled at the end of the game to determine a winner. Older students might prefer to write a title on each TV set and describe the setting, plot, and characters so the other players can guess the name of the show.

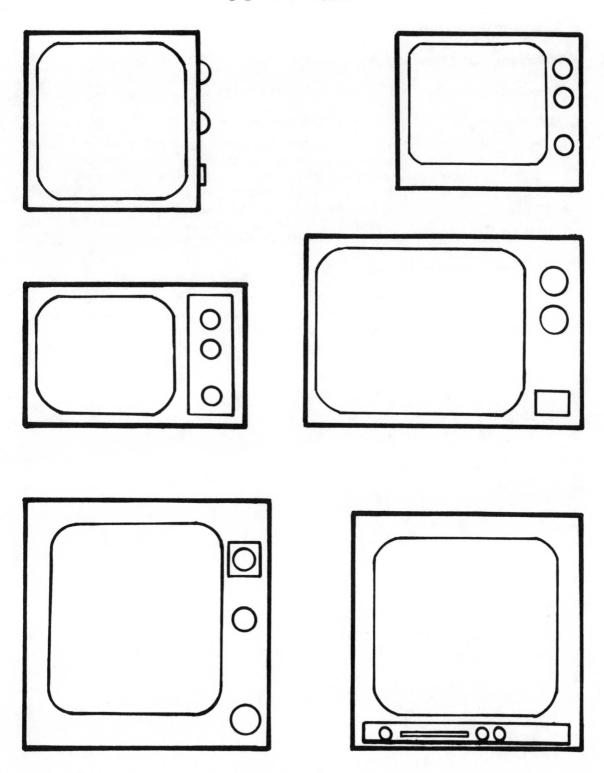

69
Sound Baseball

Suggested Grade Level: 3-8

Materials: Game sheet and pencil for each player.

Objective: The student will correctly articulate a target sound.

Method of Play

Write a stimulus word containing the target sound on each baseball. Distribute the game sheets and pencils. Players in turn select a baseball and either say the stimulus word three times or use the stimulus word in three sentences. A player who does not respond correctly receives a strike and does not score in that turn. Keep score by marking the selected baseball after a correct response. If the player responds correctly in the first or second turn, a *run* is recorded on the scoreboard and that baseball is marked off.

> *Example:*   The first player selects a baseball on which *some* is written. The player says the word three times correctly. That baseball is marked and one run is recorded on the scoreboard for the first inning. The second player attempts the same task but makes an error on the third response. The baseball is not marked off nor is a score written on the scoreboard. The score for the inning is now one to nothing, and play proceeds to the second inning.

When all nine innings have been played, the player with the highest number of runs is the winner.

INNINGS	1	2	3	4	5	6	7	8	9
TEAM 1									
TEAM 2									

SCOREBOARD

69 **Sound Baseball**

70
What's in the Boxes?

Suggested Grade Level: 3-8

Materials: Game sheet and crayons or pencil for each player.

Objectives: 1.   The student will correctly articulate a target sound.
2.   The student will improve auditory reception.

Method of Play

For Objective 1: Distribute the game sheets and crayons or pencils. Tell the players that they have received all the presents shown on the game sheets but that they may not open them until their birthdays. They may guess the contents of each box, but the guesses must contain their target sounds. The articles mentioned do not have to make sense nor do they have to fit the size of the boxes. Players take turns selecting a box and telling what might be in it. If the target sound is articulated correctly, the player draws the object on the box or writes its name on the box. The object is to mark off all the boxes.

For Objective 2: Give each player a game sheet and pencil. Tell the players that they are going to guess which box you describe. The player who guesses correctly marks the box on the game sheet. Describe one of the boxes and an object it might contain. Players take turns guessing which box has been described. The game ends when all boxes have been described.

70 What's in the Boxes?

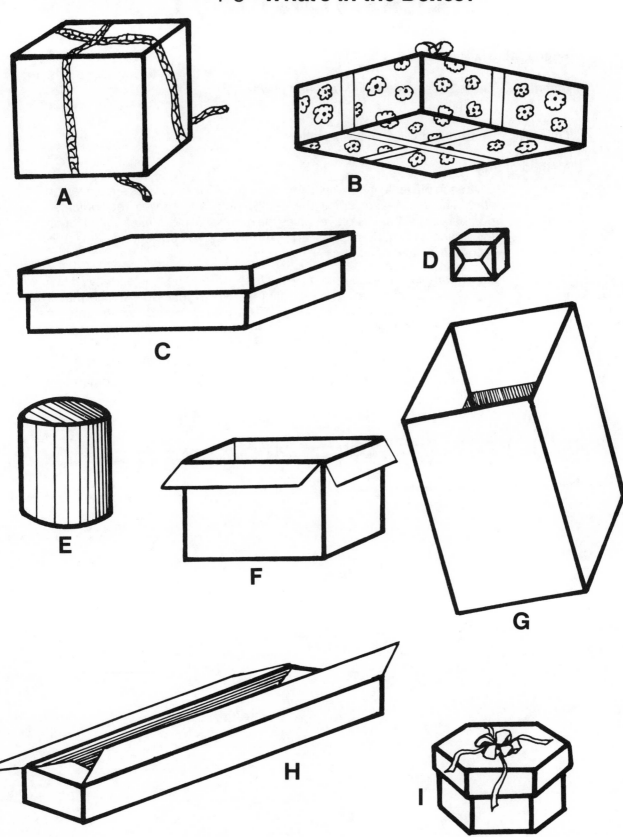

A

B

C

D

E

F

G

H

I

71
Can You Say?

Suggested Grade Level: 3-8

Materials: Game sheet and marker for each player.
1-4 Spinner.

Objective: The student will use classification.

Method of Play

Give each player a game sheet and a marker. All the markers are placed on *start.* The first player spins the 1-4 Spinner and moves the indicated number of spaces. The player gives the number of responses called for on the space the marker lands on. The number of correct responses is recorded on that space.

> *Example:* The spinner arrow stops on 2. The player moves two spaces. The stimulus is *Two wiggly words.* The player says, "worm, kitten." The player records two points on that space. The next player lands on *Three party words,* says, "Birthday, present, baby," and records only two points because *baby* is not an appropriate response.

When all players have completed the path, points are totaled to determine the winner.

Start	Three words that make you feel happy	Two wiggly words	One sad word	Three funny words
Two color words				Two noisy words
Three sweet words	71 Can You Say?			One sky word
One word that makes you think of flying				Three party words
Two words that make you think of round objects				Two school words
Three words that describe you	One word your mother says	Two zoo words	Three pretty words	One word that reminds you of a book

72
A Bright Idea

Suggested Grade Level: 3-8

Materials: Game sheet and pencil or crayon for each player.

Objectives: 1. The student will correctly articulate a target sound.

2. The student will use verbal expression.

Method of Play

For Objective 1: Give each player a game sheet and pencil or crayon. Tell the players to write or draw as many objects as possible that contain the target sound on the light bulb. Give them a reasonable amount of time. When time is up, ask each player to read the words or name the objects. One point is awarded for each correct production. The player who has the most points is the winner.

For Objective 2: Distribute the game sheets and pencils or crayons. Ask the players to draw something to represent the brightest idea they have ever had inside the light bulb. Encourage imagination and originality. Ask the players to show their drawings and tell about their bright ideas. Ask players to vote for the idea they like best. Present a ribbon or star to the winner.

Variation:

Discuss various categories of ideas with the players. Establish several different categories such as the most original, the most expensive, the most economical, the most scientific, the most helpful, the most dangerous, the most interesting, etc. Set up enough different categories so each player can be awarded a ribbon or star.

72 **A Bright Idea**

73
Dinosaur Hunt

Suggested Grade Level: 3-8

Materials: Game sheet and marker for each player.
1-4 Spinner.

Objectives: 1. The student will correctly articulate a target sound.

2. The student will use adjectives, adverbs, appropriate verb tenses, plurals, antonyms, synonyms, etc.

Method of Play

For Objective 1: Write stimulus words on the spaces on the game sheets. Distribute the game sheets and markers. All the markers are placed on *start*. The first player spins the 1-4 Spinner. The number the spinner arrow stops at indicates the number of times the player must articulate the stimulus word correctly. The player records one point for each correct production on that space. Each player moves one space at a time, responding according to the number on the spinner. When all players have reached the dinosaur, the points are totaled to determine the winner.

Variation:

Ask the players to use the stimulus words in sentences. The spinner will indicate the number of spaces the marker should move. If the spinner arrow stops at 4, that player moves four spaces, responds with a correct sentence, and remains on that space. If the production is incorrect, the player moves the marker back one space and waits for the next turn. The first player to reach the dinosaur is the winner.

For Objective 2: Write the stimulus words on the spaces. Distribute the game sheets and markers. The first player spins the 1-4 Spinner and moves the indicated number of spaces. The player responds to the stimulus on that space, and if correct, remains there. If incorrect, the marker is moved back one space and the player responds correctly to the stimulus word on that space. The first player to reach the dinosaur is the winner.

Variation:

This may be used as a classification activity. Play the game as described for Objective 1. The spinner is used to determine the number of responses per turn.

170

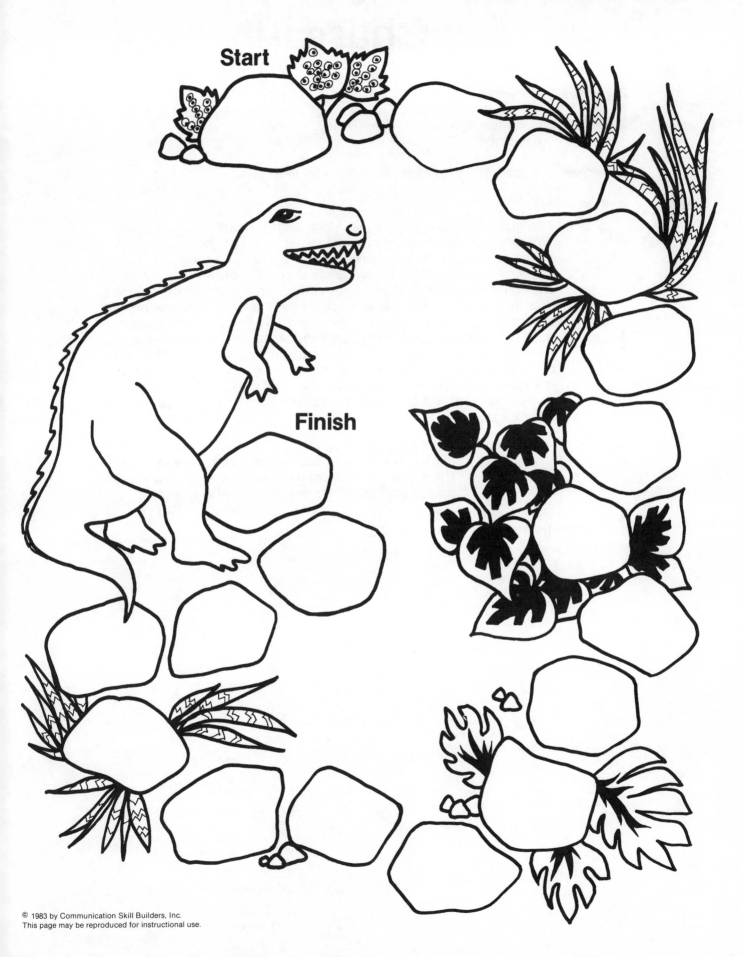

73 **Dinosaur Hunt**

Start

Finish

74
Chase

Suggested Grade Level: 3-8

Materials: Game sheet and marker for each player.
1-6 Spinner.

Objective: The student will correctly articulate a target sound.

Method of Play

Two players use one game sheet—one player at each end of the sheet. Write stimulus words containing the target sound on the spaces. Distribute the game sheets and markers. Each player places a marker in the circle on the opposite end of the game sheet. The player sitting in the 2 position of the game sheet places a marker across the sheet on the circle with the number 1. The player sitting in the 1 position places a marker across the game sheet on the circle with the 2. The object of the game is to be the first player to reach the opposite end of the game sheet. Players take turns spinning the 1-6 Spinner, moving the indicated number of spaces, and saying each word passed. When an error is made, the player stops on that space and waits for the next turn. If a player lands on a space occupied by the opponent, the opponent is "bumped" back to the starting circle and begins again.

Example: The spinner arrow stops on 3. The first player moves the marker three spaces, saying each word passed, "Share, show, sheet." The second player spins a 5 and moves five spaces, saying, "Shine, shake, shoe, shave, sharp."

The first player to reach the last space on the opposite side of the sheet is the winner.

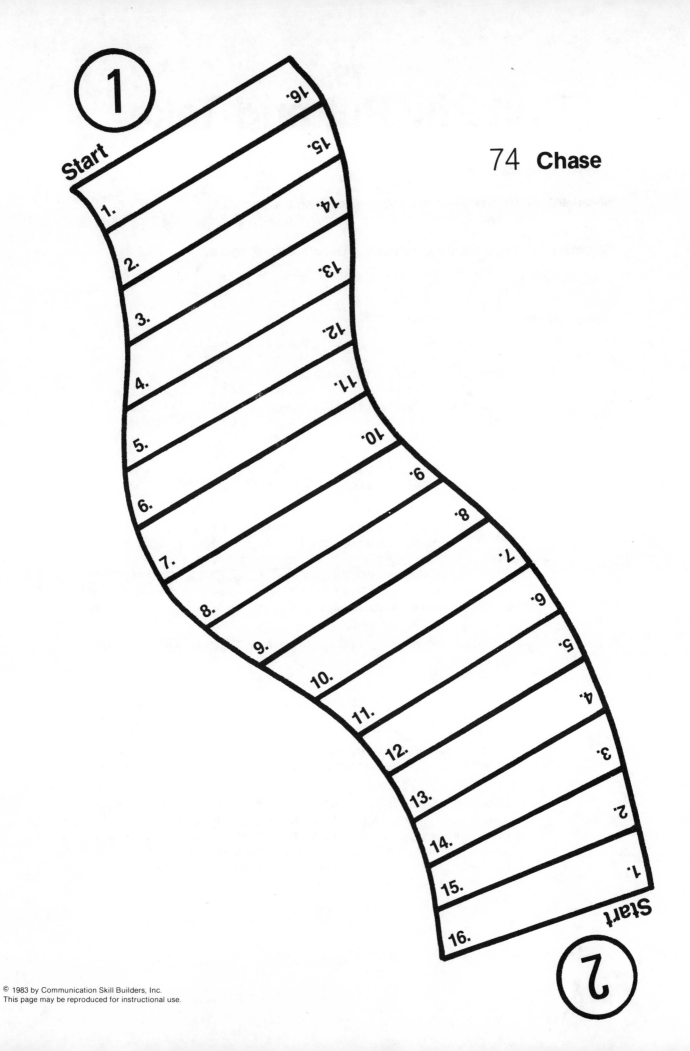

74 Chase

75
Butterfly Put and Take

Suggested Grade Level: 3-8

Materials: Game sheet and four markers for each player.
1-6 Spinner.

Objectives: 1. The student will correctly articulate a target sound.

                2. The student will use adjectives, antonyms, synonyms, plurals, appropriate verb tenses, etc.

Method of Play

For Objective 1: Give each player a game sheet and four markers. The stimuli are provided orally or on cards to be turned over by the players in their turns. The object of the game is to be the first player to place all four markers on the butterflies. The 1-6 Spinner is used to determine the number of times a player says the stimulus word and to indicate if a marker may be placed. A player spins the 1-6 Spinner and articulates the stimulus word the indicated number of times. If correct and if the spinner arrow stopped at an *even* number, the player places a marker on the game sheet. If the arrow stops at an *odd* number, the player removes *any* marker from the sheet.

Example: The first player spins a 4 (which is an even number), says the stimulus word four times correctly, and places a marker on a butterfly. The second player spins a 2 (which is an even number), says the stimulus word correctly twice, and places a marker on a butterfly. The first player spins again and gets a 3 (which is an odd number). The player says the stimulus word three times, then *removes* the second player's marker from the game sheet.

The game ends when a player has placed all four markers on the game sheet.

Variations:
Vary the game depending on the allotted time for play. For a shorter game, make the rule that markers are not removed once they are played but an odd number means the player cannot place a marker on the game sheet. For a longer game, a player removes his or her own marker when an odd number results from a spin.

For Objective 2: Distribute the game sheets and markers. The rules are similar to those for Objective 1. However, to spin the spinner, the player must respond correctly to the stimulus word. The spinner is used only to indicate if a marker may be placed on or removed from the game sheet. If a response is incorrect, the player loses a turn.

76
Hearts and Clovers

Suggested Grade Level: 3-8

Materials: Game sheet and marker for each player.
1-6 Spinner.

Objective: The student will correctly form questions and sentences.

Method of Play

Give each player a game sheet and marker. The markers are placed on *start*. The 1-6 Spinner determines the number of spaces a player moves. If landing on a space containing a clover, a player asks another player a question. If landing on a space containing a heart, the player forms a sentence following pre-established criteria. This can be a sentence of a personal nature, a descriptive sentence, or a sentence telling about an experience. If a response is incorrect, the player goes back one space and follows the signal or instructions on the new space. The first player to reach *end* is the winner.

Variations:
Pictures serve as interesting stimuli for the sentence construction task. A set of cards on which question words are written may help with forming questions.

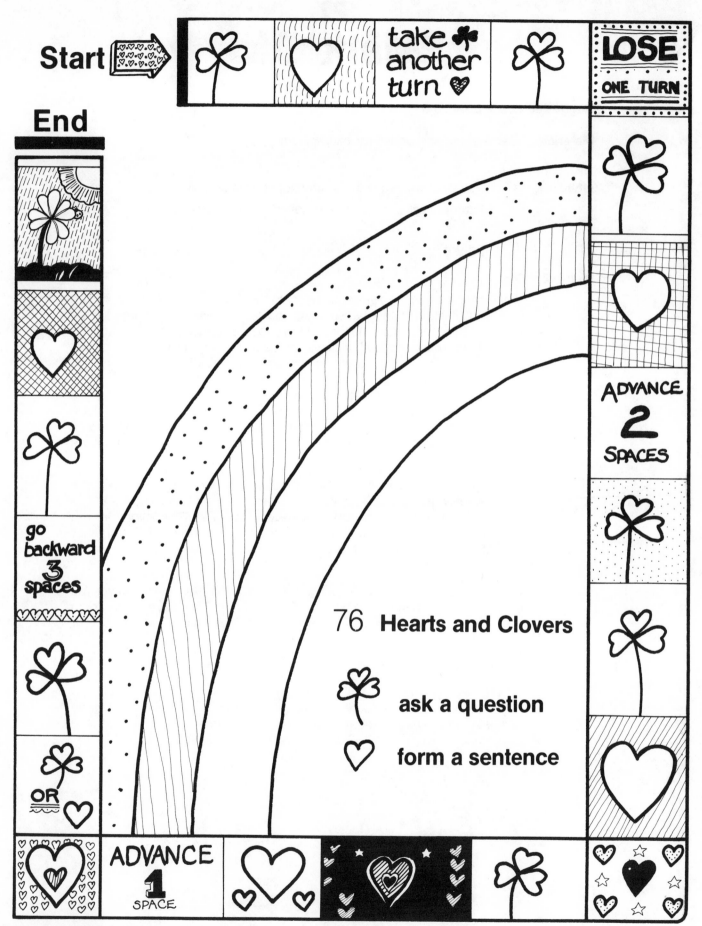

Start

End

take another turn

LOSE ONE TURN

ADVANCE 2 SPACES

go backward 3 spaces

OR

ADVANCE 1 SPACE

76 Hearts and Clovers

ask a question

form a sentence

77
Mark Off

Suggested Grade Level: 3-8

Materials: Game sheet and pencil for each player.
1-6 Spinner.

Objectives: 1. The student will correctly articulate a target sound.

             2. The student will use adjectives, adverbs, antonyms, synonyms, plurals, etc.

             3. The student will use classification.

Method of Play

For Objective 1: Write a stimulus word containing the target sound in each box. Distribute the game sheets and pencils. Players in turn spin the 1-6 Spinner twice. The total of the two numbers indicates the box the player responds to. If a player spins first a 3 and then a 7, the total would be 10 and the player responds to the stimulus in box 10. If correct, the box is marked off and the next player takes a turn. There are two 6 boxes. If neither 6 box is marked off, a player who spins a total of 6 may chose either of the two boxes. If a box has already been marked off, the player still responds to the stimulus, or the stimulus word may be used in a sentence. The first player to mark off all the boxes is the winner.

For Objective 2: Write the stimulus words in the boxes. Distribute the game sheets and pencils. Play proceeds as described for Objective 1. The first player to mark off all the boxes is the winner. When working with adjectives, the stimuli would be nouns. Players could spin the spinner three times. The third time would determine the number of adjectives to be given.

    Example: The spinner arrow stops on 3 and then 2. The player will respond to box 5 which says *dog.* The player spins again and gets 4. This means that the player provides four adjectives to describe a dog.

For Objective 3: Write a category on each box. Distribute the game sheets and pencils. Play is the same as for Objective 1, except that the players provide multiple responses to each stimulus word. This can be done by spinning the spinner a third time as for Objective 2, or by stating the requirement before beginning the game.

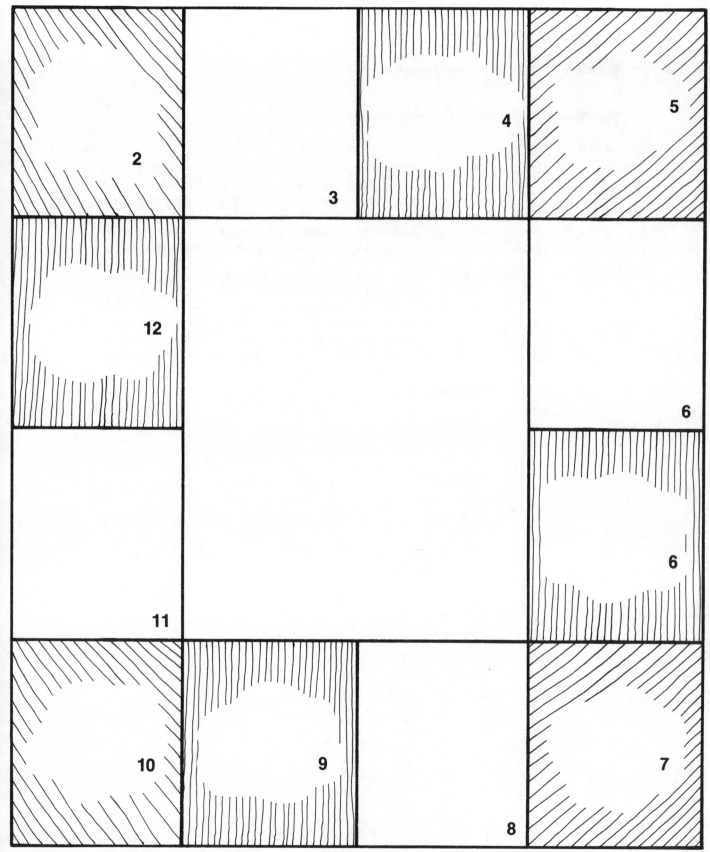

78
Smiles

Suggested Grade Level: 3-8

Materials: Game sheet and marker for each player.
1-6 Spinner.

Objective: The student will use classification.

Method of Play

Write a category on each of the nine empty spaces. Give each player a game sheet and a marker. Establish a time limit. The markers are placed on *start*. A player spins the 1-6 Spinner and moves the indicated number of spaces in either direction. A point is earned each time a player lands on a smiling face. When landing on a circle containing a stimulus word, the player responds according to the number indicated on the spinner.

> *Example:*   The spinner arrow stops at 2. The player moves clockwise two spaces. The stimulus word is *drinks*. The player says, "Milk, cola." The next player spins a 4 and moves counter-clockwise. The stimulus word is *furniture* and the response is "Chair, bed, sofa, table." Now the first player spins a 1, which takes the marker to one of the smiling faces. That player scores a point.

Play continues until time is up. The player with the most points wins the game.

Start

78 Smiles

79
Letter to Slim Jim

Suggested Grade Level: 3-8

Materials: Game sheet and pencil for each player.

Objectives: 1. The student will correctly articulate a target sound.

              2. The student will use verbal expression.

Method of Play

For Objective 1: Give each player a game sheet and a pencil. Ask the players to write a letter to Slim Jim. The players may decide that Slim Jim is a famous movie star, a long-lost uncle, a baseball player, etc. The letters may be humorous or serious. When all have been completed, the players read their letters, being careful to articulate the target sound correctly. Record a point for each correct production and note errors on the game sheets for later practice. The player with the most correct productions of the target sound is the winner.

For Objective 2: Give each player a game sheet and a pencil. Ask the players to draw a picture for or write a letter to Slim Jim. Have the pictures or letters describe a problem. They may be humorous or serious. Then the players take turns describing the problem to the other players who provide possible solutions.

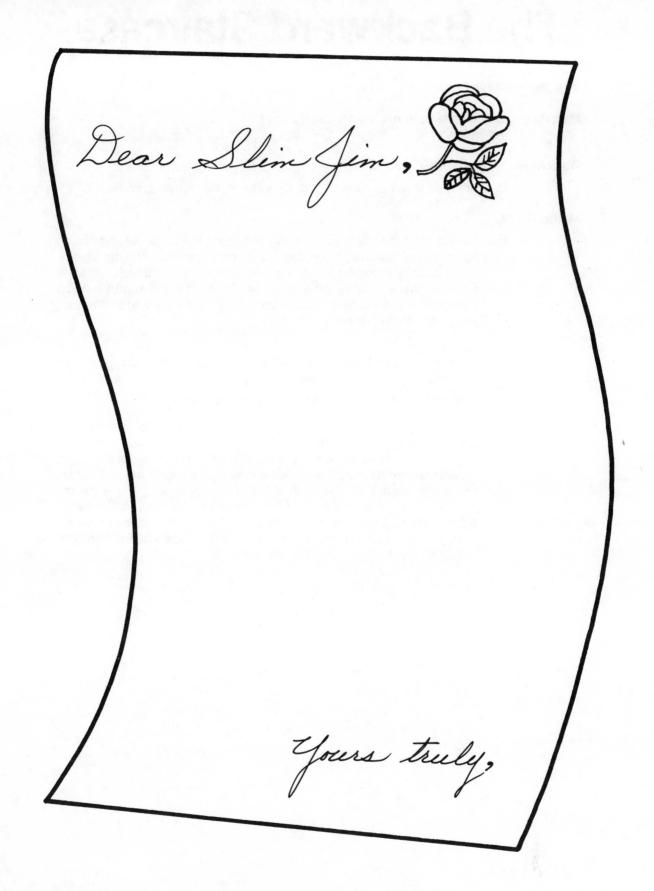

Dear Slim Jim,

Yours truly,

80
The Backward Staircase

Suggested Grade Level: 3-8

Materials: Game sheet and marker for each player.
1-4 Spinner.

Objectives: 1. The student will correctly articulate a target sound.

2. The student will use antonyms, synonyms, homonyms, verbs, etc.

Method of Play

For Objective 1: Write stimulus words containing the target sound on the steps. Distribute the game sheets and markers. Place the markers at the bottom of the staircase on *start.* Moves are determined by the 1-4 Spinner. When landing on a step, the player says the stimulus word correctly and waits on that step for the next turn. If an error is made, the player loses a turn.

Variation:
Players say the stimulus word on each step passed, stopping on a step when an error is made.

The first player to reach the door is the winner.

For Objective 2: Write stimulus words on the steps. Distribute the game sheets and markers. Place the markers on *start.* Moves are determined by the 1-4 Spinner. Players take turns spinning, moving the indicated number of spaces, and responding to the stimulus word on the space the marker lands on. If the response is correct, the player remains there, losing a turn. If the response is incorrect, the other players are given a chance to respond. With a correct response for another player's turn, a player moves one space ahead. The first player to reach the door is the winner.

184

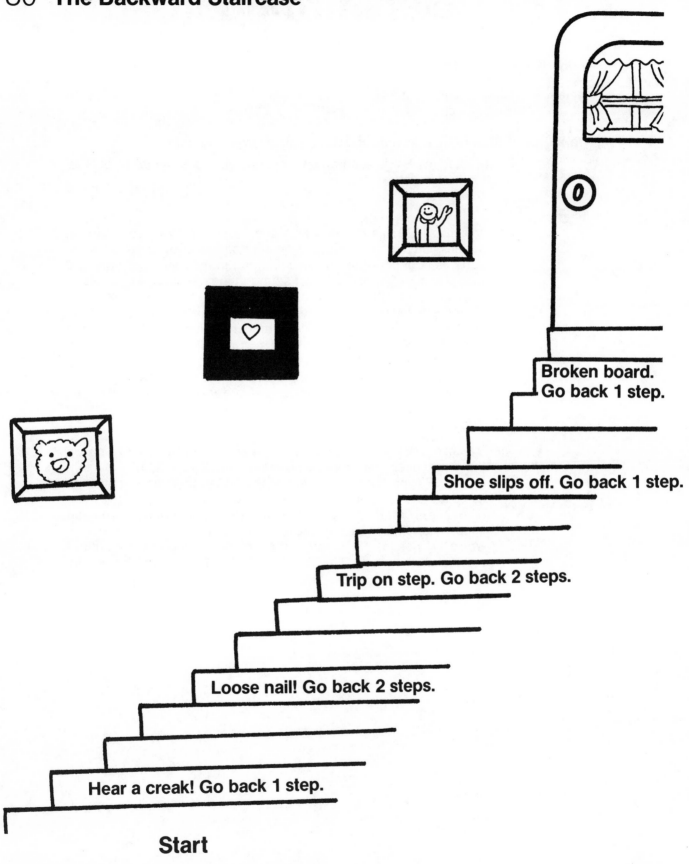

Broken board.
Go back 1 step.

Shoe slips off. Go back 1 step.

Trip on step. Go back 2 steps.

Loose nail! Go back 2 steps.

Hear a creak! Go back 1 step.

Start

81
Get in Shape

Suggested Grade Level: 3-8

Materials: Game sheet and marker for each player.
1-4 Spinner.

Objectives: 1. The student will correctly articulate a target sound.

               2. The student will use antonyms, synonyms, homonyms, adjectives, classification, etc.

Method of Play

For Objective 1: Write stimulus words containing the target sound in the shapes. Circles could have the target sound in the final position, squares could contain the target sound in the initial position, and triangles might have the target sound in the medial position. Distribute the game sheets and markers. Place all the markers at *start*. Moves are determined by the 1-4 Spinner. Players in turn spin the spinner and move the indicated number of spaces. If landing on a circle, the player says the stimulus word only once. If the player lands on a square, the stimulus word is said twice. Landing on a triangle means the stimulus word is said three times. If a response is incorrect, the player goes back one space and says the word in that space the required number of times. The first player to reach the *end* is the winner.

For Objective 2: Provide stimulus words either orally or by writing them on the game sheet. Distribute the sheets and markers. Place the markers on *start*. Players take turns spinning the 1-4 Spinner, moving the indicated number of spaces, and responding to the stimulus word. If the response is correct, the player records the number of points on that space. If landing on a circle, the player receives one point. A square is worth two points, and a triangle three points. Play continues until all players reach the *end*. The player with the most points is the winner.

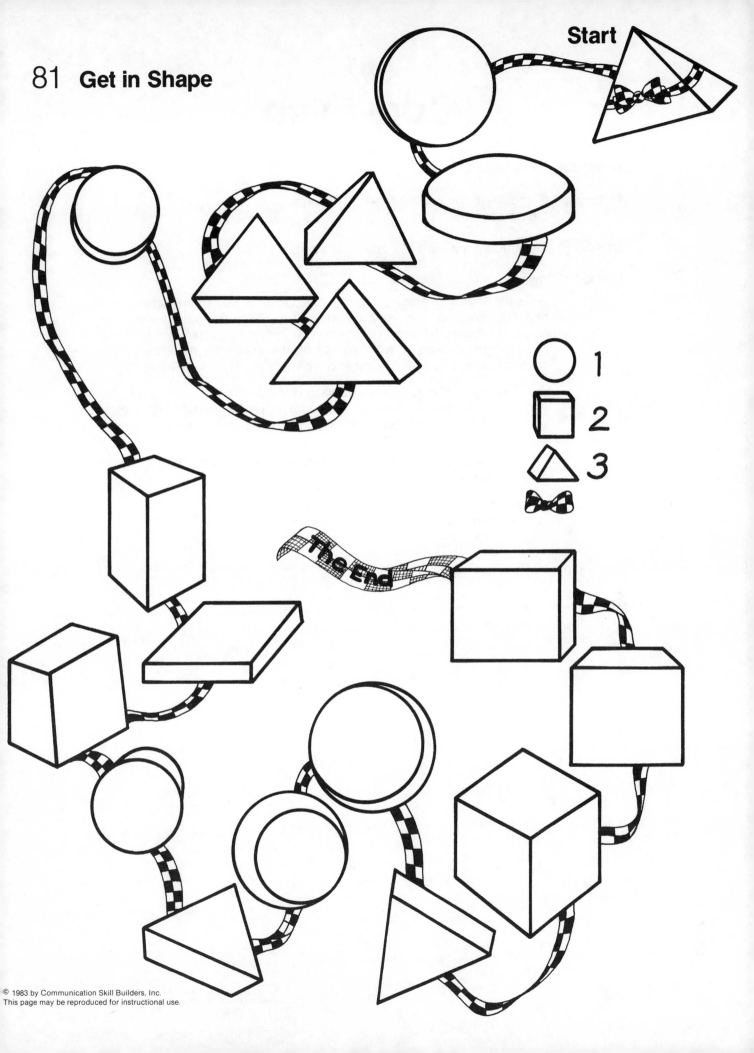

81 **Get in Shape**

Start

1
2
3

The End

82
Odd-Even

Suggested Grade Level: 3-8

Materials: Game sheet and marker for each player.
1-6 Spinner.

Objective: The student will correctly articulate a target sound.

Method of Play

Write the stimulus words on the spaces. Distribute the game sheets and markers. Place all markers on *start*. A player in turn spins the spinner twice. The first spin is for an even or odd number. An even number allows the player to move ahead while an odd number sends the player back. The second spin indicates the number of spaces the player may move.

Example: If the spinner arrow stops at 6 on the first spin and at 3 on the second spin, the player moves *forward three* spaces. If the arrow stops first at 3 and then at 6, the player moves *back six* spaces.

The spinner arrow must stop at an even number for the player to begin play. The first player to reach *end* is the winner.

Variation:
The task may require that the stimulus be used in a sentence.

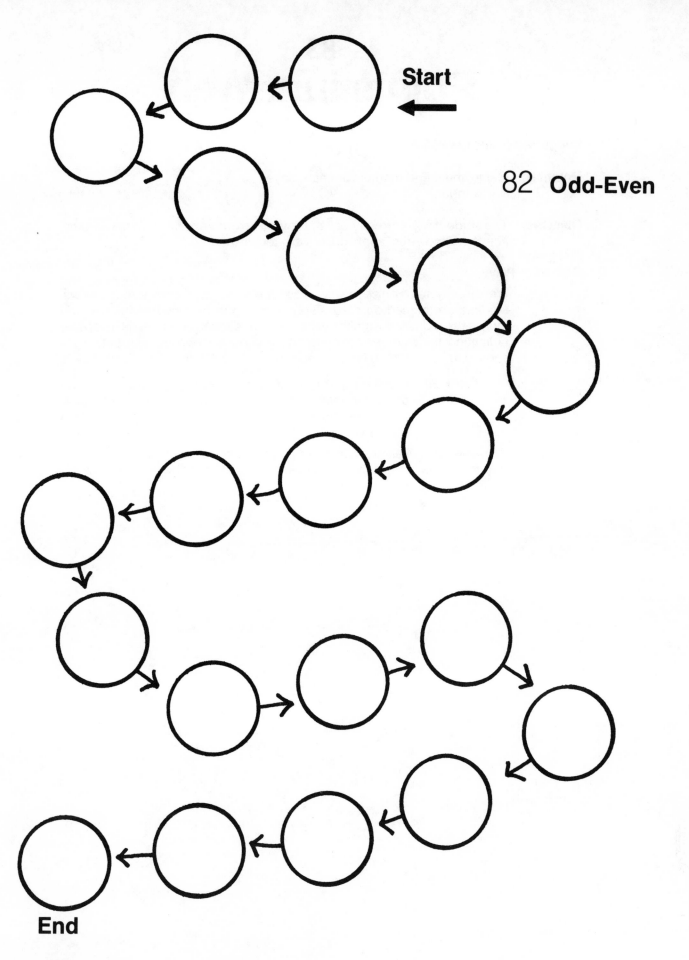

Start

82 **Odd-Even**

End

83
Points in a Web

Suggested Grade Level: 3-8

Materials: Game sheet and marker for each player.
1-4 Spinner.

Objective: The student will correctly use antonyms, synonyms, homonyms, idioms, adjectives, adverbs, appropriate verb tenses, etc.

Method of Play

Write the stimulus on each space. Distribute the game sheets and markers. Markers are placed on *start*. Each player in turn spins the spinner and moves the indicated number of spaces. On each space there is a number indicating the number of points the response is worth. The player responds, and if correct, is awarded the points on that space.

> *Example:* From *start,* antonyms written on the game may be *up, good, smooth,* and *light.* The spinner arrow stops at 4. The player moves four spaces and responds, "Dark." This is worth one point because the number on the space is 1.

If a player makes an error, another player responds. If correct, that player scores the points. All players must reach *finish* to end the game. Points are totaled to determine the winner.

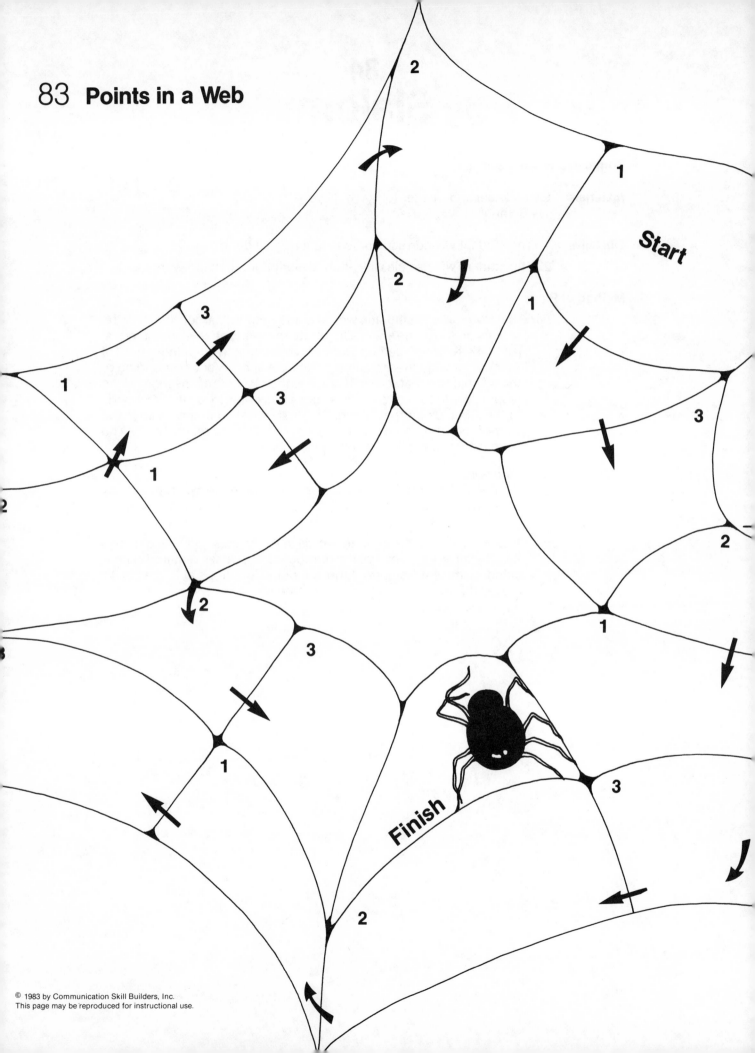

84
Slalom

Suggested Grade Level: 3-8

Materials: Game sheet and marker for each player.
1-4 Spinner.

Objectives: 1. The student will correctly articulate a target sound.

2. The student will use classification, description, rhyming words, etc.

Method of Play

For Objective 1: Write stimulus words containing the target sound in the spaces on the game sheet. Distribute the game sheets and markers. All markers are placed on *start*. Players take turns spinning the 1-4 Spinner, moving the indicated number of spaces, and responding to the stimulus on that space. If correct, the player remains there. If the response is incorrect, the player goes back one space and responds to the stimulus on that space. The first player to reach *finish* is the winner, but the game continues until all players reach *finish*. The players take first, second, third places.

Variation:

For added practice, the number the spinner arrow stops at may also be used to indicate the number of times a player is required to produce each stimulus word.

For Objective 2: Write the stimulus words in the spaces. Play the game as for Objective 1 except that the number of responses required is indicated by the 1-4 Spinner. If the spinner arrow stops at 3, the player moves three spaces and provides three responses.

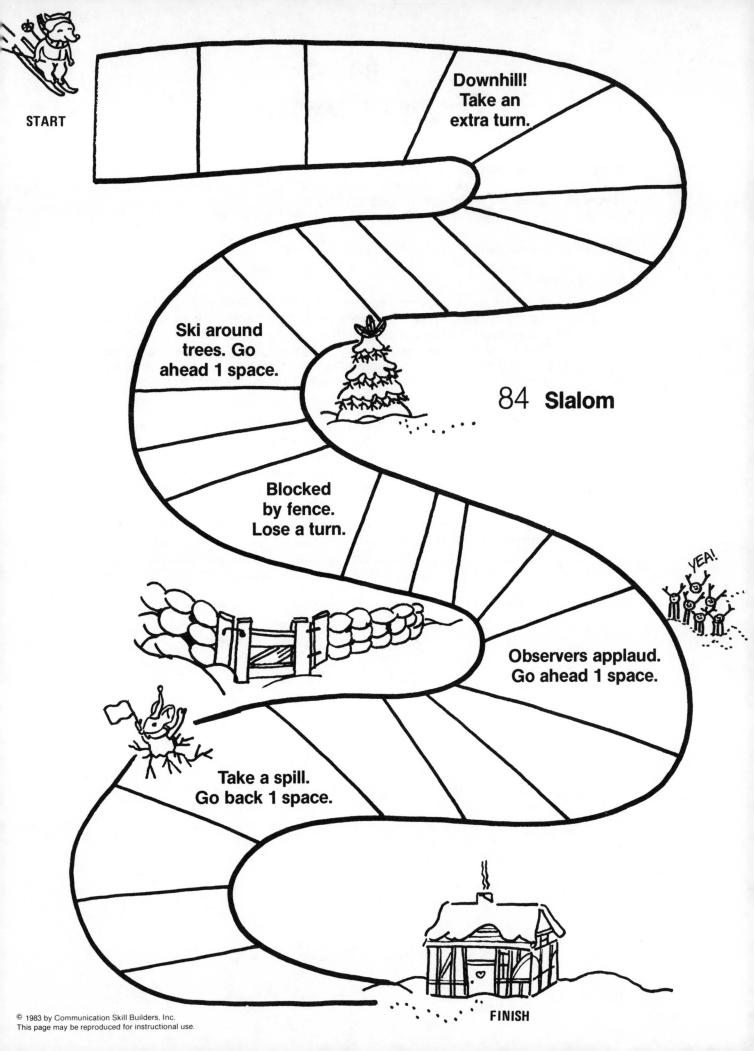

START

Downhill!
Take an
extra turn.

Ski around
trees. Go
ahead 1 space.

84 Slalom

Blocked
by fence.
Lose a turn.

YEA!

Observers applaud.
Go ahead 1 space.

Take a spill.
Go back 1 space.

FINISH

85
Town Center

Suggested Grade Level: 3-8

Materials: Game sheet and marker for each player.
1-6 Spinner.

Objective: The student will use classification.

Method of Play

Give each player a game sheet and a marker. Markers are placed on *start*. Players in turn spin the 1-6 Spinner, move the indicated number of spaces, and name items that can be bought in that store or building according to the number indicated on the spinner. If correct, the player remains on that space. If the response is incorrect or incomplete, the player moves back the number of spaces that correspond with the number of items lacking in the response.

> *Example:* The first player spins a 4, moves to the Grocery Store, and tries to think of four items that can be found in a grocery store. The player can name only three items, so moves back one space to the Hospital. Now the player must name four items that could be found in a hospital. The player then remains on that space until the next turn.

Play continues until a player reaches the end of the path and leaves town. That player wins the game.

85 **Town Center**

Entering Town

| Apartment Building |
| Bakery |
| Hospital Lose a turn. |
| Grocery Store |
| Park |
| Furniture Store |
| Parking Lot |

Leaving Town

| Golf and Tennis Club | Music Store | Book Store | Men and Boys Shop |

| Barber shop |
| Police Station Lose a turn. |
| Hobby Shop |
| Florist |
| Stationery Store |
| Dress Shop |

| Shoemaker | Drugstore | Tailor | Library Lose a turn. | Zoo | Karate Studio |

© 1983 by Communication Skill Builders, Inc.
This page may be reproduced for instructional use.

All the Games Kids Like
4-6

86
Money Game

Suggested Grade Level: 4-6

Materials: Game sheet and pencil for each player.
Plus and Minus Spinner.

Objectives: 1. The student will correctly articulate a target sound.

2. The student will use antonyms, synonyms, irregular plurals, appropriate verb tense, etc.

Method of Play

For Objective 1: Write stimulus words containing the target sound on each coin. Distribute the game sheets and pencils. Write several words or a sentence on the dollar bill. The players begin at *start* and, in turn, say the word on that coin. Players who are correct, mark their coins and proceed to the next coin. If incorrect, the player does not mark the coin before moving to the next coin. When players have reached the dollar bill, they attempt the bonus dollar. The player who correctly articulates the words or sentence on the bill is the winner. If there is more than one winner, the player with the most marked coins is the winner.

Variation:

For more repetition, this game can be played with the Plus and. Minus Spinner. A plus sign with a number means to move forward that number of coins. A minus sign with a number means to move backward that number of coins.

For Objective 2: Write stimulus words on the coins and a more difficult stimulus on the dollar bill. Distribute the game sheets and pencils. Play the game as described for Objective 1.

86 Money Game

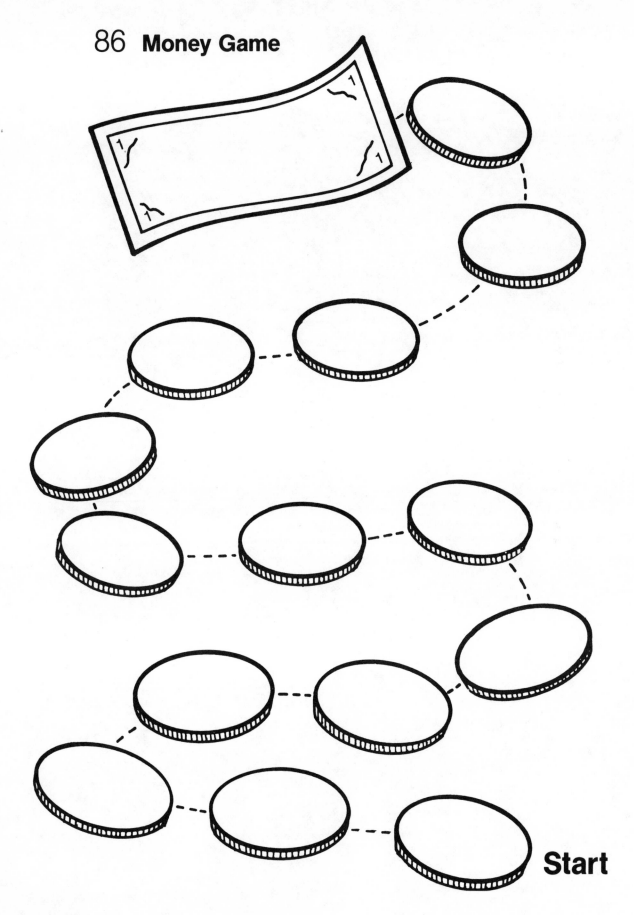

Start

All the Games Kids Like
4-8

87
Call Up

Suggested Grade Level: 4-8

Materials: Game sheet and marker for each player.
1-4 Spinner.
Real or toy telephone will provide realism for this activity.

Objectives: 1. The student will use verbal expression.

             2. The student will learn appropriate and correct telephone use.

Method of Play

For Objectives 1 and 2: Give each player a game sheet and a marker. Place the markers on *start*. The first player spins the 1-4 Spinner and moves the indicated number of spaces. The player performs the task specified on the space the marker lands on with you acting as the party being called. The game continues with players taking turns. Play ends either at your discretion or when a player returns to *start*. Encourage oral expression as well as correct telephone usage. A player landing on a space marked *Busy, Wrong number,* or *No answer* should tell what this means and what can be done about it.

Start

87 **Call Up**

Wrong number.

Call your uncle to invite him to dinner.

Call the local newspaper to get a subscription.

Call the market for an order.

Call your friend for some homework.

Call information to get a number you don't know.

Call the movie theater to see what's playing.

Call the dog pound to see if they found your lost dog.

Busy.

Call the furniture store to tell them when to deliver your new bed.

Call the post office because you're missing some mail.

Call your grandmother to see how she is feeling.

No answer.

Call the phone company to correct the bill.

Call the library to see if they have the book you want.

Wrong number.

Call the fire station to report a fire.

Call the plumber to repair a leak.

Call to order records from an ad on TV.

Busy.

Make a collect call.

Call the doctor for an appointment.

Call your Mom because you'll be late.

No answer.

88
Ad Agency

Suggested Grade Level: 4-8

Materials: Game sheet for each player.

Objectives: 1. The student will correctly articulate a target sound.
2. The student will use verbal expression.

Method of Play

For Objective 1: Give each player a game sheet. A player selects an object on the sheet, describes it, explains its potential use, and tells how it might be advertised. Players may wish to work as a group and pool ideas or they make take turns selecting items by themselves. Listen for the correct production of the target sound and record any errors on the game sheets for later practice.

For Objective 2: Give each student a game sheet. Players in turn choose an object on the sheet, describe it, tell its potential use, and tell how they might advertise it. They might be asked to compose a commercial. The players may work in groups and present their ideas as a team, or they may work individually.

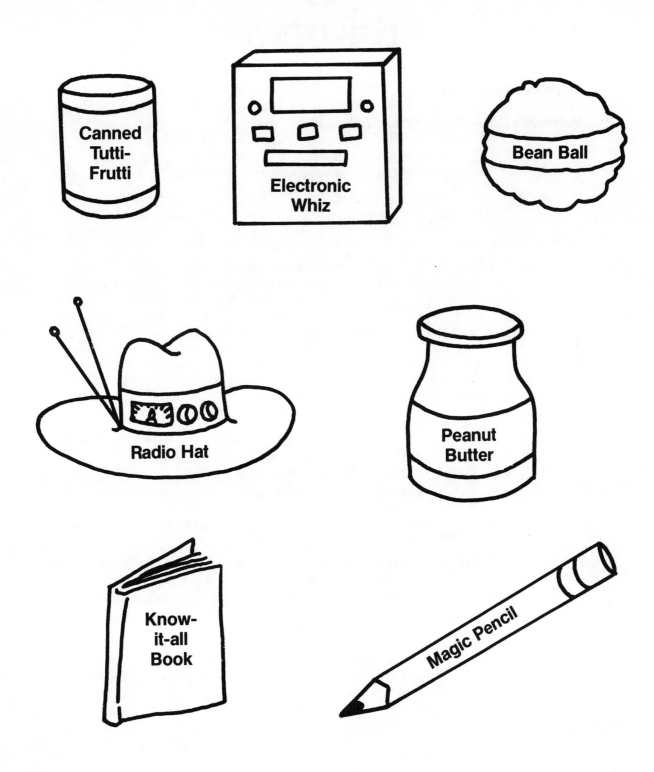

Canned Tutti-Frutti

Electronic Whiz

Bean Ball

Radio Hat

Peanut Butter

Know-it-all Book

Magic Pencil

88 **Ad Agency**

89
Reverse

Suggested Grade Level: 4-8

Materials: Game sheet and marker for each player.
1-4 Spinner.

Objectives: 1. The student will correctly articulate a target sound.

2. The student will use classification.

3. The student will use antonyms, synonyms, adjectives, etc.

Method of Play

For Objective 1: Write a stimulus word that contains the target sound on each empty space. Distribute the game sheets and markers. The markers may be placed on any space. A player in turn spins the 1-4 Spinner, moves the marker the indicated number of spaces, and responds to the stimulus word on the last space. One point is given for each correct production. If a marker lands on a space marked *Reverse,* the player takes another turn but must turn around and go in the opposite direction. Play ends at your discretion. The player with the most points is the winner.

Variation:
Have each player produce the stimulus word a given number of times and receive a point for each correct production.

For Objective 2: The game is played as described for Objective 1 except that a category is written on each space. A player spins the spinner, moves the marker the indicated number of spaces and responds to the category on the space landed on. The player names the number of items indicated by the spinner arrow.

Example: The spinner arrow stops at 4. The player moves four spaces. The category in the fourth space is *sports.* The player responds, "Baseball, skating, tennis, jogging."

Each correct response wins one point. Total the points at the end of the game to determine the winner.

For Objective 3: The game is played as described for Objective 1 but the stimuli will differ. Players provide correct responses to the stimulus words on the spaces the markers land on.

206

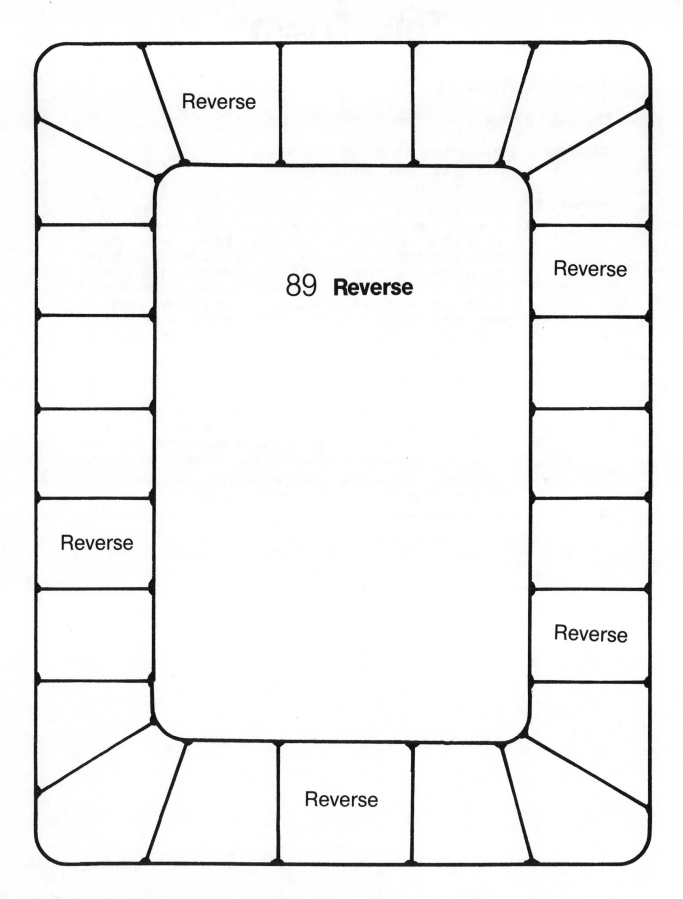

89 **Reverse**

90
Talk Town

Suggested Grade Level: 4-8

Materials: Game sheet and marker for each player.

Objectives: 1. The student will give accurate directions.

2. The student will follow oral directions.

Method of Play

For Objectives 1 and 2: Give each player a game sheet and marker. The markers are placed anywhere on *Starter Street.* The first player selects a destination on the game sheet but does not reveal it to the group. The object of the game is to provide directions that will lead the other players to the destination. Players move their markers in response to the directions. If someone reaches the destination, the player providing directions wins a point. The player who is first to arrive at the destination is the next player to choose a destination and give directions.

Example: All the markers are placed on *Starter Street.* The first player selects the gas station and says, "Go north along *Straight Street.* Stop at the first corner and then go half a block. The place I want to go to is on the left." The first player to arrive at the gas station takes the next turn directing the players to a new destination from the gas station.

Traffic signs must be obeyed. At a traffic light, the player giving directions can decide if the light is red, green, or amber. The game ends at your discretion.

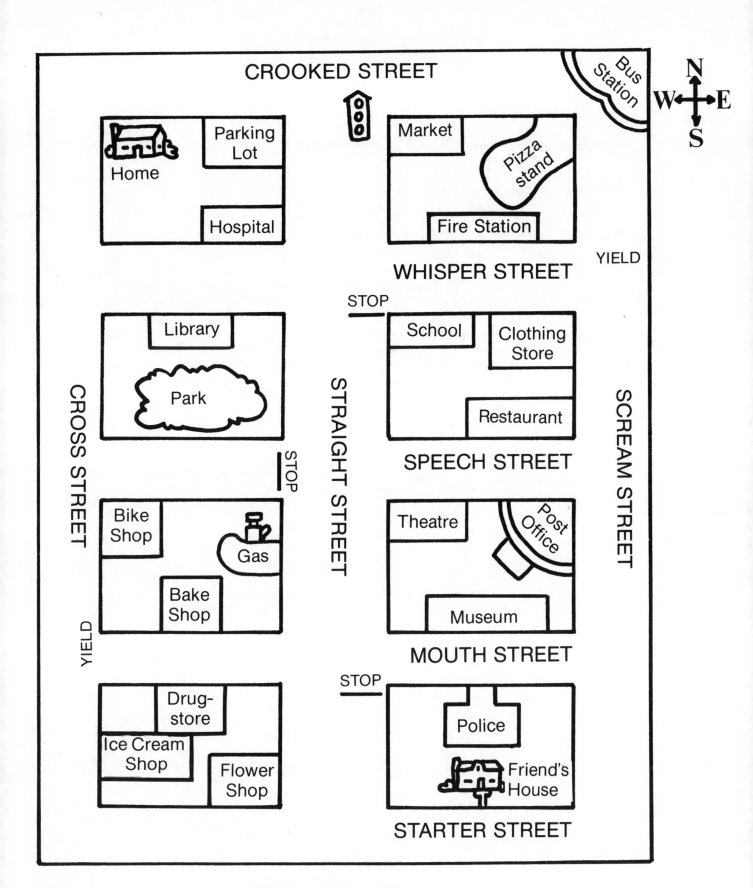

90 **Talk Town**

91
Tell-on Story

Suggested Grade Level: 4-8

Materials: Game sheet and marker for each player.
1-4 Spinner.

Objectives: 1. The student will comprehend question words.

2. The student will form questions.

3. The student will use verbal expression.

Method of Play

For Objective 1: Distribute the game sheets and markers. Each player in turn spins the 1-4 Spinner, moves the marker the indicated number of spaces, and responds to the stimulus number on the space the marker has landed on. The number 1 means *who* (a person), 2 means *what* (an object), 3 means *where* (a place), and 4 means *why* (a reason possibly beginning with *because*). If a response is correct, the player receives the number of points indicated by the spinner. The points are recorded on the player's game sheet.

Example: If the spinner arrow stops at 3, the player responds to *where* by stating the name of a place. If correct, the player receives three points.

When all players have completed the sheet, the game ends and points are totaled to determine the winner.

For Objective 2: Write stimulus words on each space. The stimuli might be nouns. The method of play is the same as described for Objective 1 except that a player forms a question that contains the stimulus word indicated by the number of the space.

Example: The space landed on has the number 3, indicating a *where* question. The stimulus word on that space is *lady.* The player asks, "*Where* did the *lady* go last night?"

For Objective 3: Inform the players that they are going to tell a continuation story. Give each player a game sheet and a marker. A player in turn spins the spinner, moves the marker the indicated number of spaces, and tells one sentence of a story using the appropriate question word.

Example: A player lands on a 4 space, indicating the word *why.* The player says, "Nobody knew *why* the boy went out in the rain." Another player spins, moves the marker to a 2 space, and says, "The boy knew *what* he wanted and was going to the old house."

The story continues in this manner until the game sheet is completed.

Ask if any of the players can summarize the story.

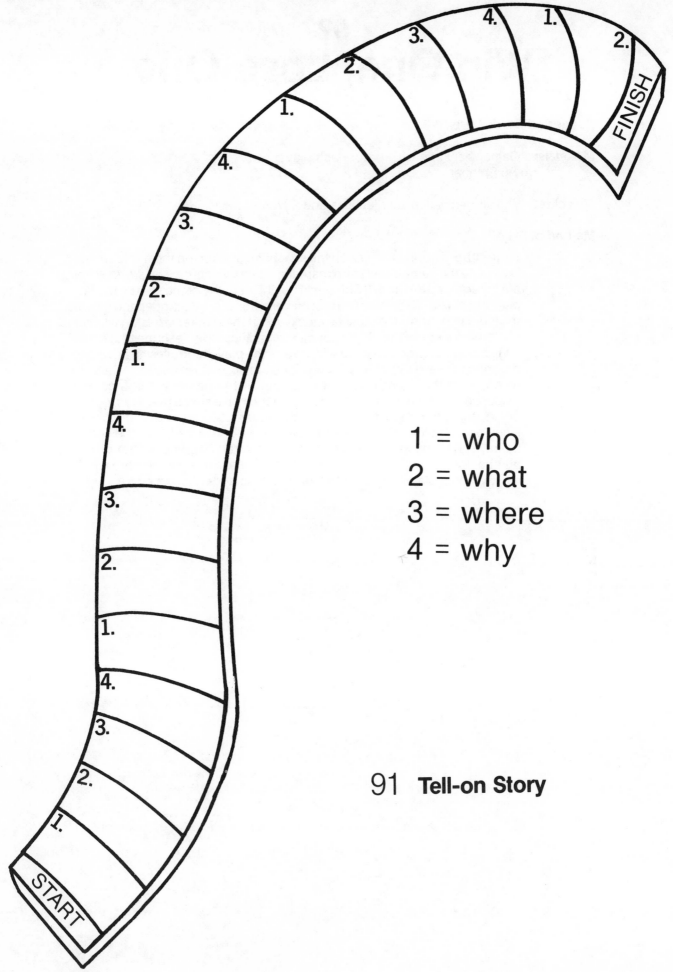

1 = who
2 = what
3 = where
4 = why

91 **Tell-on Story**

92
Win One, Lose One

Suggested Grade Level: 4-8

Materials: Game sheet and marker for each player.
1-6 Spinner.

Objective: The student will use adjectives and adverbs.

Method of Play

Write either a noun or a verb on the spaces so marked on the game sheets. Distribute the game sheets and markers. Place the markers on *start*. Moves are determined by the 1-6 Spinner. The object of the game is to be the first player to collect 20 points. The first player spins the 1-6 Spinner and moves the indicated number of spaces clockwise. If the marker lands on a space containing a noun, the player supplies an adjective to describe that noun. If the marker lands on a space with a verb, the player supplies an adverb to describe the verb. A point is scored for each correct response. Points are recorded in the score box at the bottom of the game sheet. Incorrect responses do not earn points. If a player lands on a space that says, *Lose 2 points,* two points are erased from the player's scoreboard. If the player lands on a space that says, *win 1 point,* one point is added to the scoreboard. Play stops when a player has accumulated 20 points, although this number may be adjusted. It is also possible to have a negative score (-1, -3, etc.). When a player passes *start,* one point is added to the score.

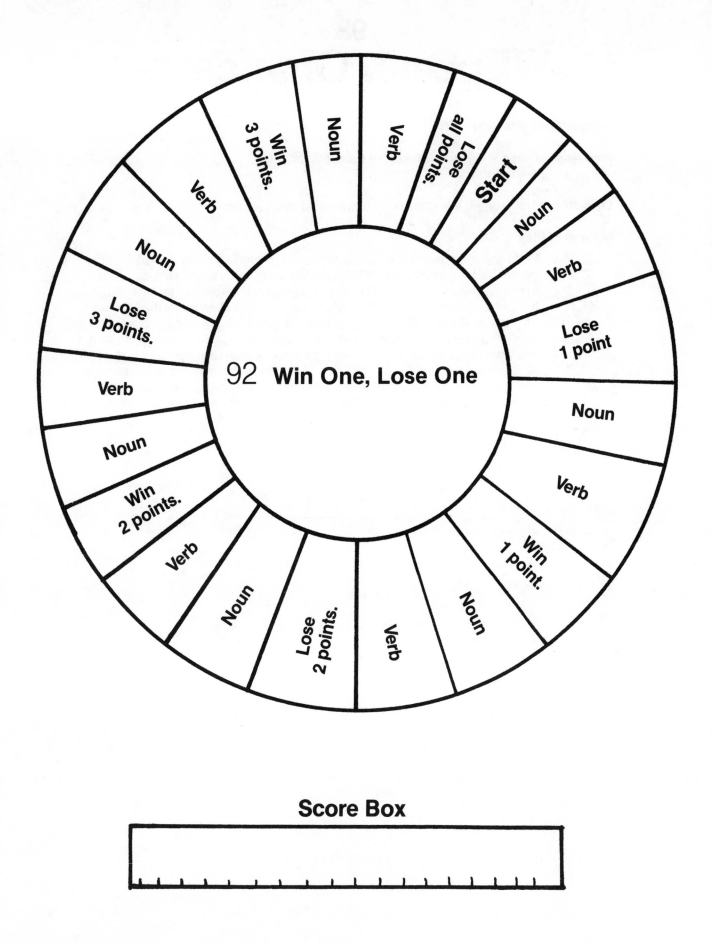

92 Win One, Lose One

Wheel segments (clockwise from Start):
Start · Noun · Verb · Lose 1 point · Noun · Verb · Win 1 point. · Noun · Verb · Lose 2 points. · Noun · Verb · Win 2 points. · Noun · Verb · Lose 3 points. · Noun · Verb · Win 3 points. · Noun · Verb · Lose all points.

Score Box

93
Speech Chance

Suggested Grade Level: 4-8

Materials: Game sheet and marker for each player.
1-4 Spinner.

Objective: The student will correctly articulate a target sound.

Method of Play

Write stimulus words in the squares on the game sheets. Distribute the game sheets and markers. Place the markers on *start*. Moves are determined by the 1-4 Spinner. The first player spins the spinner and, staying in the same square, moves to the side of the square indicated by the spinner. The player then enters the adjacent square. A marker can cross into another square only if the number indicated by the spinner is on the line shared by the two squares. As soon as a new square is entered, the player says the target sound in that square. If the response is correct, the player remains in the new square. If the response is incorrect, the player must return to the old square. The first player to reach *the end* is the winner.

93 Speech Chance

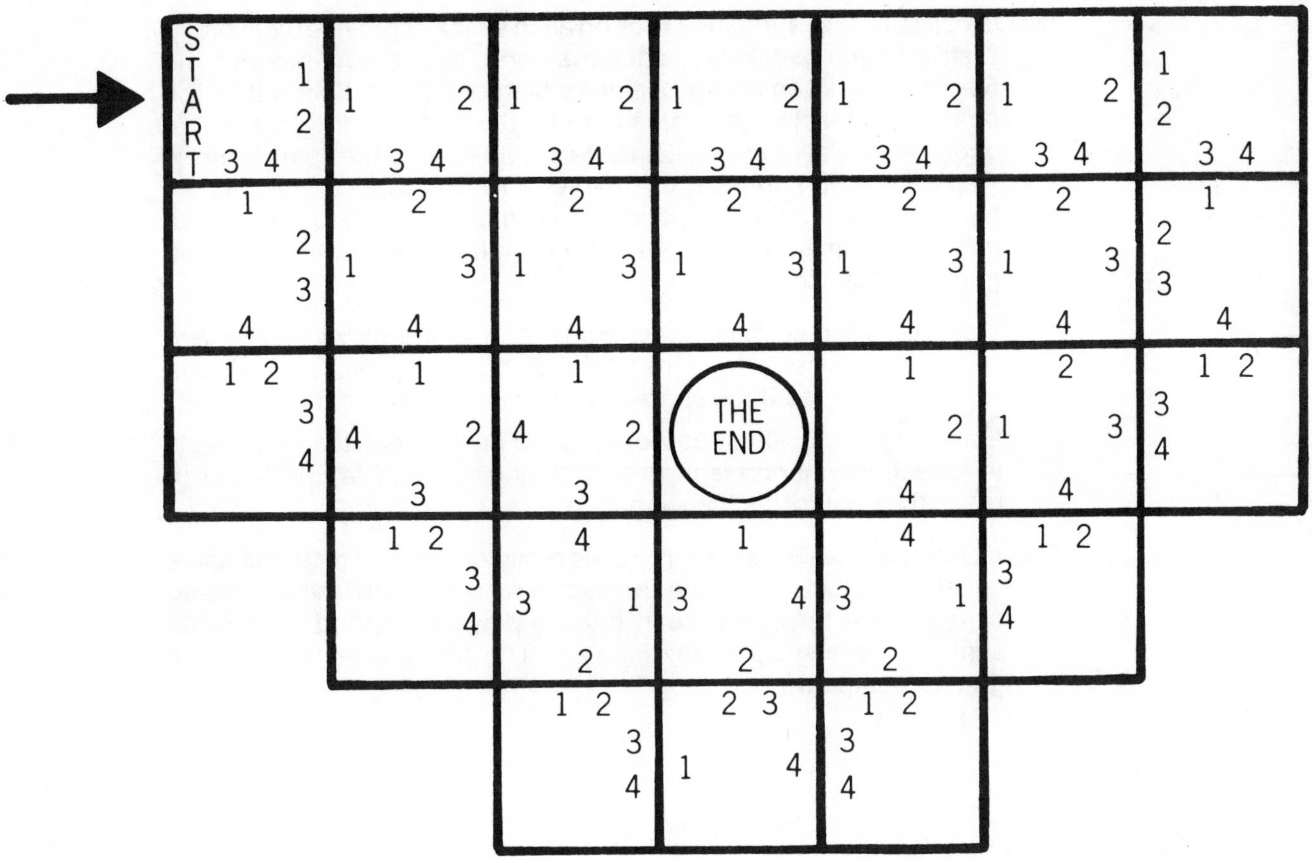

START game board with the following numbered squares:

Row 1:
- S T A R T 1 2 / 3 4
- 1 2 / 3 4
- 1 2 / 3 4
- 1 2 / 3 4
- 1 2 / 3 4
- 1 2 / 3 4
- 1 2 / 3 4

Row 2:
- 1 / 2 3 / 4
- 2 / 1 3 / 4
- 2 / 1 3 / 4
- 2 / 1 3 / 4
- 2 / 1 3 / 4
- 2 / 1 3 / 4
- 1 / 2 3 / 4

Row 3:
- 1 2 / 3 4
- 1 / 4 2 / 3
- 1 / 4 2 / 3
- THE END
- 1 / 2 / 4
- 2 / 1 3 / 4
- 1 2 / 3 4

Row 4:
- 1 2 / 3 4
- 4 / 3 1 / 2
- 1 / 3 4 / 2
- 4 / 3 1 / 2
- 1 2 / 3 4

Row 5:
- 1 2 / 3 4
- 2 3 / 1 4
- 1 2 / 3 4

94
Speech Super Bowl

Suggested Grade Level: 4-8

Materials: Game sheet and marker for each player.
1-4 Spinner.

Objectives: 1. The student will correctly articulate a target sound.

2. The student will use antonyms, synonyms, homonyms, idioms, and selected vocabulary, etc.

Method of Play

For Objective 1: Write stimulus words on each space or provide them orally. Distribute the game sheets and markers. Place the markers on the 50-yard line. Each player decides which end of the field will be the goal. The object of the game is to be the first player to reach that goalpost. A player in turn spins the 1-4 Spinner. If the spinner arrow stops at an even number, the marker is moved *toward* the goalpost the indicated number of spaces. If the spinner arrow stops at an odd number, the marker is moved *away* from the goalpost the indicated number of spaces.

Example: The spinner arrow stops at 2 so the player moves two spaces toward the goalpost. The next player spins a 3 and moves three spaces away from the goalpost.

Players say each stimulus word passed on the field. If a response is incorrect, the marker is moved back one space. The first player to reach the goalpost is the winner.

For Objective 2: Give the stimulus words orally or write them on the game sheets. Distribute the game sheets and markers. This game is played as described for Objective 1, but the players respond only to the stimuli on the spaces they land on. The first player to reach the goalpost is the winner.

94 Speech Super Bowl

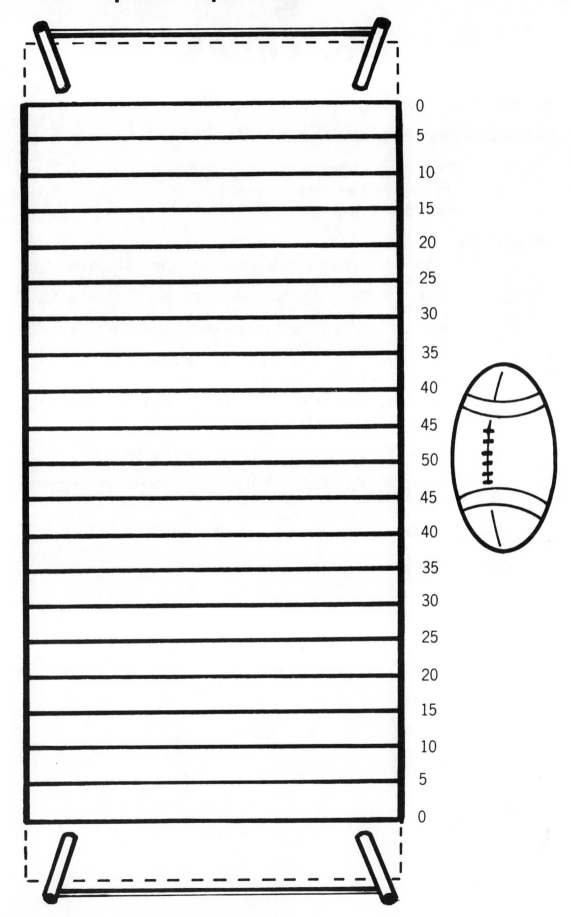

95
The Times

Suggested Grade Level: 4-8

Materials: Game sheet and pencil for each player.

Objectives: 1. The student will correctly articulate a target sound.
2. The student will use verbal expression.
3. The student will form questions.

Method of Play

For Objective 1: Tell the players that they are reporters writing their "big stories." Give each player a game sheet and pencil. Instruct them to design a headline and perhaps illustrate the story on the game sheet. Headlines must contain the target sound. When these tasks are completed, the stories are told and the illustrations shown. Chart the productions as the stories are told. Points may be given for each correct production. Note any incorrect productions on the game sheets for further practice.

For Objectives 2 and 3: This activity can provide a means for evaluating language production as well as for eliciting verbal expression. The players pretend to be reporters trying to write prize-winning stories. Distribute the game sheets and pencils. Each player writes a story with a headline. The stories may also be illustrated. If more space is needed, ask the players to turn their game sheets over. Then the players take turns relating their stories. After each story is told, the other players each ask a question of the reporter. You may require that the questions begin with a specific question word.

The TIMES

96
Fortune Cookies

Suggested Grade Level: 4-8

Materials: Game sheet and pencil for each player.
If players have not seen fortune cookies, have some on hand to display and discuss before working on this activity.

Objectives: 1. The student will use verbal expression.

                 2. The student will learn idioms or proverbs.

Method of Play

For Objective 1: Give each player a game sheet and pencil. Ask the players to think of sayings that might be in fortune cookies. Players take turns presenting their ideas to the group and then writing them on the game sheet. The sayings may be humorous or serious, may be within a given framework, or may be sentences using a particular structure such as future tense or plurals. Play ends when all the spaces have been used.

For Objective 2: Write an idiom or proverb on each space on the game sheet. Each player might have a set of idioms or proverbs that are different from the others. Distribute the game sheets and pencils. Each player selects a fortune and explains the idiom or proverb or uses the idiom in a sentence. If correct, that space is marked off. The player who defines or uses the most expressions correctly wins the game.

96 **Fortune Cookies**

97
Progress

Suggested Grade Level: 4-8

Materials: Game sheet and marker for each player.
1-6 Spinner.

Objective: The student will correctly articulate a target sound.

Method of Play

Write stimulus words in each space on the game sheet. Distribute the game sheets and markers. Place the markers on *start*. Players in turn spin the 1-6 Spinner and move horizontally or vertically to an adjacent space. Diagonal moves are not allowed. In order to move, the number indicated by the spinner arrow must correspond to the number on one of the adjacent spaces and the response to the stimulus word in that space must be correct.

> *Example:* The first player's marker is on *start*. The spinner arrow stops at 1. The player may move up or to the right to either space marked 1. The player chooses to move horizontally to the space on the right. On the next turn, the player spins a 3. The marker cannot be moved as the nearest 3 is located diagonally. On the next turn, the arrow stops at 2. The player moves to the space above. The next time around, the player spins a 6 and again moves to the space above.

Play continues, each player taking a turn, until one player reaches *end,* which requires a spin of 1, 3, or 4 to enter.

> *Variation:*
> The spinner may also be used to determine the number of times the player is to say the stimulus word.

2	1	2	**END** 1, 3, or 4
3	4	5	6
4	3	2	1
1	3	5	4
3	2	4	6
2	1	6	5
1	6	5	4
1	2	3	4
START	1	2	3

97 **Progress**

98
Multiply Your Strength

Suggested Grade Level: 4-8

Materials: Game sheet, marker, and pencil for each player.
1-4 Spinner.

Objectives: 1. The student will correctly articulate a target sound.
2. The student will define words, idioms, or tell the meaning of proverbs.

Method of Play

For Objective 1: Write stimulus words containing the target sound on each space. Distribute the game sheets and markers. Place the markers on *start.* Players in turn spin the 1-4 Spinner and move the number of spaces indicated. The player must provide a correct response to the stimulus word on the space landed on. If correct, the player receives the number of points on that space multiplied by the number indicated on the spinner.

Example: The spinner arrow stops at 3. The player moves three spaces, uses the stimulus word in a sentence and articulates the target sound correctly. The number on that space is 3 and the number indicated on the spinner is 3. The player multiplies the two numbers and earns nine points. The second player spins a 4, moves four spaces, and responds correctly. The number on the space is 3 so the second player receives 12 points.

Play ends when all players have reached *end.* The player with the most points is the winner.

For Objective 2: Write the stimuli on the game sheet, placing the more difficult on the spaces giving the most points. The game is played as described for Objective 1, but the players must define or explain words, idioms, or proverbs. After all have completed the game sheet, the player with the most points is the winner.

224

End

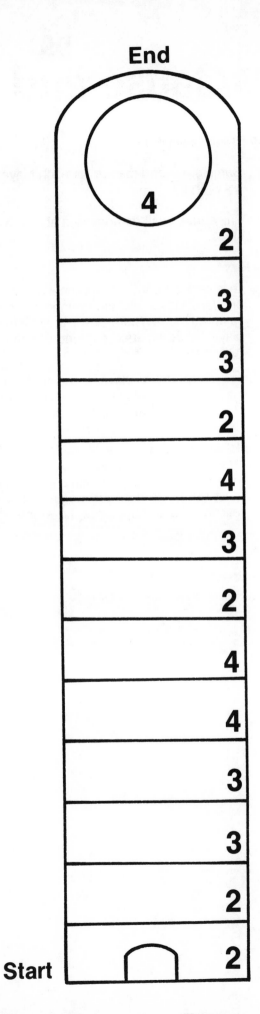

4

2

3

3

2

4

3

2

4

4

3

3

2

2

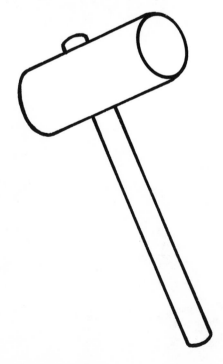

Start

99
Cause and Effect

Suggested Grade Level: 4-8

Materials: Game sheet and marker for each player.
1-4 Spinner.

Objective: The student will demonstrate ability to equate cause and effect relationships.

Method of Play

Give each student a game sheet and a marker. All the markers are placed on *start.* Moves are determined by the 1-4 Spinner. Players take turns spinning the 1-4 Spinner and moving the indicated number of spaces. The player reads the effect sentence the marker lands on and states a possible reason for that effect.

> *Example:* A player lands on the space that says *His finger hurt.* The player must give a logical reason for the hurting finger and state it in acceptable grammatical form, such as, "His finger hurt because he cut it with a knife."

If the response is not acceptable, the player misses a turn. No two players may occupy the same space at the same time. The first player to arrive on the space is "bumped" when another player lands on the same space and must return to *start* and begin again. Play continues until one player reaches *end* and becomes the winner.

| The police came. | The bird flew away. | The car did not start. | His finger hurt. | The tire was flat. | The toast burned. | Start |

| The dog barked. |
| The baby cried. |
| The lights went out. |
| He got a new suit. |
| The groceries spilled. |
| She couldn't open the door. |

| The baby fell down. | They lost the game. | The crackers were stale. | She didn't eat lunch. | They woke up early. | She couldn't cut the meat. | End |

100
Syntax Spin

Suggested Grade Level: 4-8

Materials: Game sheet and pencil for each player.
1-6 Spinner.

Objective: The student will ask a question, differentiate between an adverb and a verb or an adjective and a noun, and produce a pair of homonyms, antonyms, or synonyms.

Method of Play

Give each player a game sheet and a pencil. Establish a time limit. Players take turns spinning the 1-6 Spinner and referring to the number on the game sheet that corresponds to the number indicated on the spinner.

Example: The spinner arrow stops at 3. The first player must *Say a pair of antonyms.* The second player spins a 1 and the task would be to *Ask a question.*

If the response is correct, the player receives the number of points stated on the space. The player records the points won after each turn. When the time is up, the player with the most points is the winner.

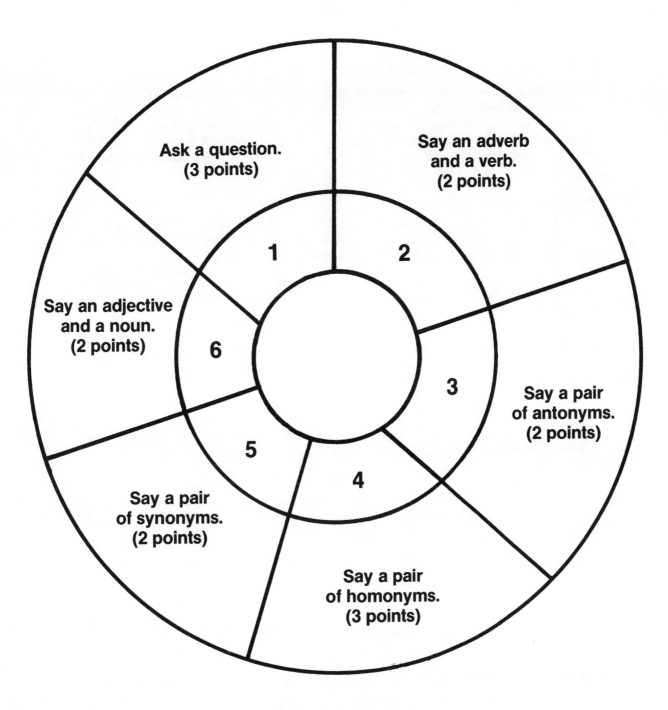

100 **Syntax Spin**

OTHER MATERIALS BY DIANNE SCHOENFELD BARAD . . .

WORDS AND SOUNDS AHOY! (1983)

A cornucopia of language and articulation games! These reproducible "bingo" cards provide a multitude of activities. You can offer versatile language games for classification, association, building vocabulary, and more. You'll also present enjoyable articulation activities for 11 target sounds. You can use this familiar game format for effective home carryover, too.   **No. 4692-Y $15.95**

SPEECH NEWS (1983)

Here's a noncompetitive language activity modeled on radio and TV broadcasts. Sixty reproducible newscasts give important carryover practice for **S, R, SH, CH,** and **J.** Also proven effective for language therapy, dysfluency, and voice therapy.
                                         No. 3135-Y $16.95

MORE VERSATILE PUBLICATIONS FROM COMMUNICATION SKILL BUILDERS . . .

PICTURES, PLEASE! An Articulation Supplement (1983)
PICTURES, PLEASE! A Language Supplement (1979)
by Marcia Stevenson Abbate and Nancy Bartell LaChappelle

Two volumes of reproducible clear line illustrations hold more than 2,000 pictures. You can photocopy each page of drawings over and over again for an unlimited variety of activities. Both of these binders are tab-indexed and all pictures are cross-referenced — you can easily find the illustrations you need.

Pictures, Please! An Articulation Supplement	No. 2091-Y	$39
Pictures, Please! A Language Supplement	No. 3092-Y	$39

TWISTER TALK (1983)   *by Debbie Harrison*

You can provide intensive articulation drill and at the same time offer stimulating language materials for older students. Your students will be entertained and motivated when they create humorous tongue twisters using **S, R,** and **L.** Colorful sentence cards and gameboards for a variety of games.   **No. 4617-Y $19.95**

ASSIST ONE, TWO, THREE (Combined and Revised, 1983)   *by Octavia Milton*

Now the popular *Assist* series is combined into one convenient volume . . . 126 reproducible articulation activities for class, clinic, and home. Individual worksheets feature games, speech riddles, stories, and pictures. Photocopy these pages for effective home carryover. Sounds included are **F, V, G, K, S, Z, R, SH, CH, TH,** and **S, R,** and **L Blends.**
                                         No. 4696-Y $24.95

Communication Skill Builders

3130 N. Dodge Blvd./P.O. Box 42050
Tucson, Arizona 85733
(602) 323-7500

All the Games Kids Like
Spinner Boards

DIRECTIONS FOR ASSEMBLING SPINNERS

1. Cut out each spinner and arrow.

2. Punch a hole in the center of each spinner and arrow.

3. Insert a brass paper fastener through the spinner and arrow, and fasten.

4. For durability, laminate the spinner boards and arrows before assembling.